THE MINISTRY OF THE CHURCH
The Image of Pastoral Care

JOSEPH J. ALLEN

THE MINISTRY OF THE CHURCH
The Image of Pastoral Care

"And we give thanks unto Thee for this ministry which Thou dost vouchsafe to receive at our hands..."

(The Anaphora of St John Chrysostom)

ST VLADIMIR'S SEMINARY PRESS

CRESTWOOD, NEW YORK 10707

1986

Library of Congress Cataloging-in-Publication Data

Allen, Joseph J.
  The ministry of the church.

  Includes index.
  1. Pastoral theology—Orthodox Eastern Church.
2. Orthodox Eastern Church—Doctrines. I. Title.
BX341.6.A44   1986   253   86-22037
ISBN 0-88141-044-6

THE MINISTRY OF THE CHURCH
The Image of Pastoral Care

© Copyright 1986

by

ST VLADIMIR'S SEMINARY PRESS

ISBN 0-88141-044-6

PRINTED IN THE UNITED STATES OF AMERICA
BY
ATHENS PRINTING COMPANY
New York, NY 10018

With love and gratitude to my wife Joan
and my sons Phillip and Joseph
and
In honor of the Twentieth Anniversary to the Episcopacy
of my father in Christ, Metropolitan PHILIP Saliba

Table of Contents

Foreword

We take this opportunity to express our sincere joy at seeing a book on ministry to enrich the library of spiritual and pastoral interest. We see in this work a first step toward considering the pastoral ministry as being primary in the life of the Church and in theological disciplines. This, in our opinion, is an important turning point away from the more speculative priorities in theological curricula and towards the existential and human—towards the thinking of not only *Who saves* but *who is saved.* Of course there has always been a chapter on Orthodox Anthropology in our theological books, but the discussion generally remained on the rhetorical, intellectual, rational level.

The pastoral life is not a superficial level of work but is the most existential. We have discovered that if man is the object of salvation, theology by definition must be to a great extent pastoral. God has written His gospel of love and reconciliation upon the face of every human being. A true pastor knows how to read and study the face of man and learn from it about God as He is revealed most perfectly.

It is high time that we come to an understanding of our religious life as being life sanctified by the coming of the Holy Spirit in the sacraments, the conduits for the sanctification of the entire cosmos. The sacraments are man-directed, man-oriented, and this is the true pastoral emphasis. We would even dare to say that the structures of the Church must be directed towards meeting people, talking with them, communicating to them the Word of God, joining them in the atmosphere of the gifts of the Holy Spirit, asking for blessing with them; because it is mainly through human beings that the transfiguration of creation takes place.

We bless Father Joseph Allen and pray that his book will be a step forward in the expected development of the field of pastoral theology which is left to the new generations of Orthodox theologians.

† IGNATIUS IV
Patriarch of Great Antioch and all the East

Pentecost
June 2, 1985

Preface

This is a study of *The Ministry of the Church*. Special emphasis throughout the study is laid upon the first word of that title, ministry. The inspiration for such a study comes immediately from Our Lord Jesus Christ: "I came not to be ministered unto, but to minister" (Matthew 20:28 and Mark 10:45). As is sometimes done, if one exchanges the two times that Our Lord used the word "minister" (διακο-νῆσαι) with the word "serve," there comes a very particular way to understand ministry: to minister is to serve.

There are those who have written about the ministry of both clergy and laity, in various perspectives. For example, some excellent theological sources on the ministry of the clergy, or on the "priesthood" in general, are to be found with an emphasis on the liturgical, historical, scriptural, doctrinal, etc., aspects, and according to the training, motivation and intent of the writer. Although one will find in these pages information taken from each of these aspects, the parameters are clear: the information is clustered around ministry, around service. Nothing more, nor less, is intended.

The author is a priest in the Orthodox Church, whose perspective, because of that faith, will be obvious to all who read these pages. However, it must be made immediately clear that this study was written to have a true value to both Orthodox and non-Orthodox Christians, and even more, to both clergy and laity.

This study is a simple study in its intent and format. Since among all the theologians with an Orthodox or Eastern Christian background, none have written about the Church with such a focus on the ministry, my prayer and hope is that this study will find its contribution.

Special thanks must be given to Metropolitan Philip through whose "persistent urging," from start to finish, I determined to undertake this work. Secondly, to my dear colleagues and fellow faculty members at St Vladimir's Orthodox Theological Seminary, Rev Paul N. Tarazi, Professor of Old Testament and Rev Basil Essey, Lecturer in Byzantine Music for proofreading, and to Constance Tarasar, Lecturer in Christian Education for the immense job of technical editing. Finally, to Lorraine Arida for her many hours of typing, and to my wife Joan, and sons Phillip and Joseph, for their patience.

JOSEPH J. ALLEN
1986

Introduction

The Ministry: Always the Same, Always Varied

The nature and meaning of the word "ministry" has taken various shapes throughout Christian history. To some it has come to denote a function only of the "clergy"—the priest, the pastor. To others the meaning has been so generalized, so emptied of its distinct character as a function of the Church, that it becomes less than a Christ-like endeavor; the one who "ministers" well, is the pleasant human being, the good social worker, the kind humanist—and even in certain countries (especially the Eastern European countries), it implies a governmental position, e.g. "The Minister of Agriculture." Still others call the leader of their Christian parish, "The Minister," which has the pious ring of "The Preacher," "The Reverend," "The Parson," etc.; this is quite foreign to those who understand the position of the shepherd, i.e. the leader and pastor of a parish, as a "fatherly" one. For these, the pastor is called "Father," and they who serve their *own* ministry as "the people of God" (laity), are members of that family of which he *is* the father.

Whatever the case may be, however it has developed and whatever radical responses it has elicited, there remain many deficient views and a distinct lack of the full understanding of the term *ministry.*

What must be said from the start is this: *ministry means service.* In a sense, that is *all* it means. Whether one is in the ministry of the clergy or of the laity, it means only that he is to serve as one appointed by God. If the word "disciple" means the "called," the "listener," the "learner," then the one who ministers is to be a *disciple* called by God. If the

13

word "apostle" means "sent," then the minister is to be an *apostle* sent by God. And if the one who ministers is a disciple and apostle, then it is also clear that this ministry, as service, is that of the *Church's* ministry. There is no true ministry which is not that of the Church, for the Church is Christ's Body in the world.

Within the Church, however, it is also clear that such ministry takes a variety of forms; it does not belong solely to either the priest or the lay person. St Paul makes this clear when writing to the Christians at Corinth:

> Now there are varieties of gifts, but the same Spirit; and there are varieties of services, but the same Lord; and there are varieties of working, but it is the same God who inspires them all in every one. (1 Cor 12:4-5)

And then he adds:

> To each is given the manifestation of the Spirit for the common good.   (1 Cor 12:7)

The First Epistle of St Peter drives the point home for us: the grace of God, which is always the same, i.e. always His grace and always given through the Spirit, is given as a varied grace.

> As each has received a gift, employ it for one another, as good stewards of God's varied grace.   (1 Pet 4:10)

These fundamental facts are known and explored by those who, in recent years, have been engaged in various joint documents, statements, consultations, etc. between various Christian bodies. In such dialogues, the subject of "ministry" is central. An excellent summary of these documents, given in a distinct Orthodox perspective, can be found in an article by Mr John Erickson entitled, "Eucharist and Ministry in Bilateral and Multilateral Dialogue."[1] Erickson's central

---

[1]"Eucharist and Ministry in Bilateral and Multilateral Dialogues," by John Erickson in *St Vladimir's Theological Quarterly*, No. 4, Vol. 28, 1984.

point—that the eucharistic model is the ideal mode for understanding the Church's ministry ("the Church's structure, including its ministry, must be fully transparent to its nature and ultimate goal, as revealed in the eucharist")—raises the preliminary question for our exploration: how can the contemporary ministry continue to adequately and responsibly express the Church's very nature and purpose in the world, without merely perpetuating "structures of antiquity?" (or as Erickson's closing comment puts it: without falling prey to "the charms of an ecclesiastical 'Williamsburg' ").[2]

Other contemporary literature is seeking to express this same concern regarding the ministry.[3] Each of the many studies seem to purport that ministry—or some insist on its plural form, "ministries'—is (are) *functional.* This does not mean that the "offices" (bishop, presbyter, deacon) can be in any way reduced to this or that function, but that each ministry exists to fulfill a specific function in, of, and for the Church. Of course, one must immediately add that the ministry of the Church cannot be identified merely with an "office," and since the laity also have a ministry, it is likewise true for them: their ministry is also—and always—functioning to accomplish what the Church is seeking to accomplish in herself and for the world.

It is constantly stated and restated, however, that there is an absolute need for public ordination to the offices; this is expressed in one or another form in most of the contemporary literature. First, the root of the word ordination, *ordo,* provides an understanding of an ordered, canonical

---

[2]This same approach is taken by Edward Schillebeeckx in his *Ministry: leadership in the community of Jesus Christ* (New York, Crossroad, 1982), where he proposes that although ministry is "to keep the community on Apostolic lines," the specific form and function of that ministry is largely a pastoral question to be determined by need, cultural content and historical discernment. (p. 18)

[3]Cf. Cooke, Bernard: *Ministry to Word and Sacrament* (Philadelphia, Fortress Press, 1976), O'Meara, Thomas: *Theology of Ministry* (New York, Paulist Press, 1983), and Chirico, Peter: "Pastoral Ministry in a time of priest shortage," in *The Clergy Review* (No. 3, March 1984). This last source emphasizes that "One ministry must always exist no matter what the circumstances of time and place. This is a unifying ministry. It co-ordinates, facilitates, gives common direction and purpose to all other ministries and to the actions of the faithful" (p. 82).

provision for permanency, stability and a public character essential to the life of the Church. Secondly, this public ordination to the offices is given as a *sacrament,* and as such, the offices are symbolic of the prophetic, leading, teaching and sanctifying nature of the Church. Those in the sacramental offices, then, are the "embodiment types" who are precisely to "embody" within themselves, in a radically focused way, the fundamental task of the Church. If those outside these offices (laity) are "ordained" to minister, that ministry comes forth from their Baptism, i.e. the baptismal commission (certainly a type of ordination) to "put on Christ." Taken together, the combined function of these two "ordinations" can be seen in an Orthodox Christian perspective. We can now make such an introductory statement if we briefly summarize the applicable points made by various prominent theologians who have done such extensive work in this area of ministry, three of which are Edward Schillebeeckx, Bernard Cooke and Thomas O'Meara.[4] Using such studies, we are able to discern the following group of functions which are generic to Orthodox ministry: (1) ministry is doing something, (2) for the advent of the kingdom, (3) expressed in public, (4) realized in such forms as witnessing, celebrating, guiding and teaching, (5) given in behalf of the community [in leadership and prophecy], (6) is a gift (charism) grounded in the faith of either baptism or ordination to an office. These six generic functions are always to be present, despite the historical variability, the mutations and even the anomalies which abound in the history of the Church. Our study will be exploring these generic functions of ministry from both an historical and contemporary view.

Finally, in terms of this introduction to our study, what must be said is that the ministry of the Church—always the same because it is God's, always varied because it is distributed differently to each one—has called us to inquire into its very nature, into the fundamental principle which energizes it and gives it its true content. Thus, in our effort to unfold the nature of ministry, we have discovered that, when

[4]*Ibid.* See references 2 and 3.

all the evidence is in, one cannot inquire about ministry without first inquiring what it is that God, as Father, Son and Holy Spirit, has done and continues to do in the life and history of mankind. God's ministry—what he has done and continues to do—is nothing less than to "reveal and reconcile"; God reveals who he is, and reconciles the world to himself. Every act of God's revelation, whether at creation, or in Christ, or by the Spirit, is his way of calling us to himself in reconciliation, speaks of who he is, tells us "a word about God." And what is the precise definition of the word "theology"? It means a "word about God." Thus, theology is truly the handmaid of ministry, and in fact, we can even say that theology, precisely as a "word about God," is born out of God's ministry, for we can only know of God what he himself has decided to reveal to us in his ministry.

From this paradigm of God's ministry, and given these introductory facts, we can see that the nature and practice of *our* ministry, whatever the context, remains intrinsically a theological activity. This ministry, then, this service which is theological, is a service *of* God, offered *to* God, and *in behalf of* God through his Church: it is *God's* service to his creation in which we participate. Thus, in our most human ministry, always the same, always varied, we are but continuing his service, his ministry.

PART I

MINISTRY TO
THE COMMUNITY

For every high priest, taken from among men, is ordained for men in things pertaining to God, that he may offer both gifts and sacrifices for sins. (Heb 5:1)

CHAPTER ONE

Christ the Great Shepherd

1. Ministry of the Shepherd: Scriptural Roots

The ministry of the shepherd is the ministry of leadership. To shepherd is to lead. In light of this understanding, however, two points must be stated. First, although there is certainly the ministry of the *laity* (cf 1 Pet 2:5 and Rom 12:1) and that "ministry" truly belongs to all members of the Body of Christ, the term "shepherding" points to the specific function of the *clergy,* e.g. the presbyters. Thus, the term "shepherd," throughout this study, refers only to the function of the priest (the clergy) who leads and pastors the community. Secondly, the Holy Scriptures, the primary source of the Church, will be relied upon, as far as is possible, rather than on any secondary sources. During this study of the term "shepherd," we shall discover within the scriptures, a clear pattern that reveals a most cohesive picture of the meaning of that term.

Of all the terms which fall within the scope of ministry, it is "shepherd" which is the most inclusive. To minister to a community is to "shepherd the flock." This is a metaphor used throughout the Old and New Testaments.

In the Old Testament, Isaiah speaks of the Lord God who will come with a strong hand; "He will feed his flock like a shepherd" (Is 40:11). Ezekiel adds: "As a shepherd seeks out his flock when some of his sheep have been scattered abroad, will I seek out my sheep; and I will

21

rescue them from all places where they have been scattered
on a day of clouds and thick darkness" (Ezek 34:12). And
later in Ezekiel: "And I will set up over them one shepherd, . . . and he shall feed them: he shall feed them and
be their shepherd" (Ezek 34:23).

In the New Testament the book of Hebrews offers a
prayer which includes the fact that "our Lord Jesus (is)
the great shepherd of the sheep," which God rose up from
the dead (Heb 13:20). Again, in Peter: "For you were
straying like sheep, but have now returned to the Shepherd
(ποιμένα) and Guardian (ἐπίσκοπον) of your souls" (1
Pet 2:25). Christ himself uses this metaphor in the gospel
according to St John: "but he who enters by the door is the
shepherd of the sheep . . . the sheep hear his voice and he
calls his own sheep by name" (Jn 10:2-4).

However, with Christ, we are dealing with something
more than a metaphor. Christ declares himself to be in
actual fact, and in no way metaphorically, The Shepherd.
"Truly, truly, I say to you, I am the door of the sheep . . . I
am the good shepherd; I know my own, and my own know
me . . . there shall be one flock, one shepherd" (Jn 10:7-16).

It is therefore Christ's ministry as the shepherd which
is the basis for all "shepherding" that takes place in his
body, the Church. Thus, we need to see just how Christ is
the shepherd, and then, what that ministry as shepherd
means in the contemporary ministry of the priesthood.

2. The Priesthood of Christ and the Ministry of the Church

Christ's shepherding is not limited to "good words and
proper teachings," although these are included. Rather it
deals with his very person and act, i.e. what he is, and did,
and continues to be and do in his Body. This "being" and
"doing" is realized by what the book of Hebrews calls "the
High Priest over the house of God" (Heb 10:21 KJV) and
again, in which "He became a High Priest of the good
things to come" (Heb 9:11 KJV).

Here the term "priesthood" enters not because it is different than Christ's "ministry," but because it stands in the center, is the core, of his ministry as shepherd of the flock. As will be seen, "priesthood" is a term which is meant to be used in a very particular way, and which can be located within the broader understanding of ministry as service. This is the priesthood proper of Christ, and this must now be clarified.

To understand this "priesthood," one can begin by using two of Our Lord's statements as they relate to his ministry in the gospel of St Mark and St Luke. "The time is fulfilled, and the kingdom of God is at hand; repent, and believe in the gospel" (Mk 1:15). Christ's ministry has been associated with these words which he spoke at the beginning of his public life. But beside this call for "repentance and belief," there is another call, a call which is tender and direct, and in which one can speak of his "priesthood" in relation to his flock. "Fear not little flock, for it is your Father's good pleasure to give you the kingdom" (Lk 12:32). In this statement, the "little flock" and the "Kingdom" are drawn together by the "Father's good pleasure." What can this mean for us? This second call concerns Christ's "priesthood," since it deals with the offering of himself as the sacrifice, i.e. with his "self-oblation." Obviously, the "Father's good pleasure" which gives to the "little flock" the "Kingdom," is found not only in his words, but in the very person and act of Christ himself, given because "God so loved the world" (Jn 3:16). Christ comes to inaugurate the Kingdom; Christ takes us into the Kingdom. When Christ is with us, the Kingdom is with us; in a sense, his act and person *is* the Kingdom as we can know it in our lives.

Thus, if it is the "Father's good pleasure" to give the "little flock" the "Kingdom," then he gives it precisely when he gives Christ himself, i.e. not merely in what he says and teaches, but in all that Christ does in his self-offering. This is his "priesthood" which stands at the center of his "ministry"; it is realized not by offering any other sacrifice, e.g. as in the Old Testament priesthood when the blood of bulls and goats are offered many times; rather, "we have been sanctified through the offering of the body of Jesus Christ once and for all" (Heb 10:10). He offers himself and is, therefore, both the one who is sacrificed and who offers the sacrifice, or as the liturgical words of the Orthodox Church say it, *the Offerer and the Offered.* Thus, through his sacrifice, the Kingdom is made present by the "Father's good pleasure."

This understanding of Christ's priesthood has a direct connection to his Church and her ministry, i.e. the ministry of his flock. Indeed, this can be seen when one notes the sequence which occurs from his call to discipleship at the beginning of his public life, up to the priestly offering of his own self.

The scripture tells us that right from the start, Jesus set about to restore the people of God by choosing disciples, and by gathering around himself a community which recognized him as the Messiah, thus recognizing itself as a messianic community, "working for the Kingdom of God." His ministry, and in turn their ministry, was direct and personal. For three years, before he would "offer his body," his ministry indeed took the shape of preaching the Kingdom, of summoning all to repentance, of seeking and saving the lost, of healing the sick and forgiving sin, of teaching those who had ears to hear, of feeding them with the bread of life, of satisfying them with living water, and of raising the dead. In this way, his ministry molded a community, a "flock," which rested upon the good news which he himself was; his flock knew—at least partially—that his person and work were the same (this, of course, would only become totally clear when the Holy Spirit was granted to them at Pentecost).

From that initial call, the Church's ministry is one and the same with Christ's ministry, which is fully realized in his high priestly act of self-oblation. And if Christ's ministry is one of self-oblation, then the Church's ministry is also one of self-oblation; it is a ministry given in the body and blood "which is broken (and) ... shed, for you and for many for the remission of sins" (*The Orthodox Liturgy*; cf also 1 Cor 11:24-25).

From this we see that the Church's ministry is not merely some "externally caused" ministry which began with Christ and which his "little flock" imitates and continues; the flock's ministry is his very own life and work—his "priesthood"—as we can know it today, i.e. he is in it and is its very source. T. F. Torrance makes this clear when he shows that the ministry of Christ on earth became identified with the human community which bears His name:

Because the person and works of Christ, what He was and what He did, are inseparable, what the Church is in Him and what it does in proclaiming Him, its being and its ministry, are inseparable. As there is only one Christ and only one Body, so there is only one ministry, that of Christ's Body.[1]

Thus, it can be said that this "one ministry" cannot be limited to a mere perpetuation of what Christ taught; it is a true organic relationship. The Church's ministry rests upon Christ's very person and being as the Son of God who became flesh in history. Not only did he teach, but his very life, death and resurrection, his ascension into heaven, etc., is itself the "thing taught"; here we see that with Christ, the lesson and the teacher of the lesson are one and the same. His person is what he teaches to this community. This is how he is the "shepherd" [who] lays down his life for the sheep" (Jn 10:11). Georges Florovsky states:

The Church is in Him. The Church is not merely a community of those who believe in Christ and walk in his commandments. She is a community of those who abide and dwell in him and in whom he himself is abiding by the Spirit.[2]

---

[1]T. F. Torrance, "The Foundation of the Church," *The Scottish Journal of Theology*, XVI (1963), p. 131.

[2]Georges Florovsky, "The Church: Her Nature and Task" in his *Collected Works*, Vol. 1, p. 60. Nordland, 1972.

Torrance adds:

> The Church of the New Covenant arose out of the
> indivisible union of the Messiah and the People of
> God He came to redeem and raise up; it grew out of
> the concrete way in which He lived His divine life
> within their human existence, thereby transforming
> their whole way of life; it took shape and form in
> every act that He performed and derived its essential
> structure from the way in which He fulfilled His min-
> istry on their behalf.[3]

It must be concluded from this that the Church's ministry, one with Christ's ministry, is fully revealed already in
the Incarnation in which God gave to us his person and
act—His "ministry to the flock"—in human history.[4]

3. Christ's Ministry as Prophet, King, Priest

In searching the scripture one finds many names at-
tached to Christ, by which he calls himself: "I am" the Light,
the Door, the Bread, the Vine, the Way, Truth and Life.
Each one describes who Christ says he is, in the famous "I
am's" of St John's Gospel. Each tells us that he is doing
more than comparing himself with these "predicates"; he
is what he is *in* these predicates; he is what takes place in
these predicates; he is describing himself as a person who is
never other than his "office" as the Christ, who *is* what he
does; his person and task are one. Thus, Christ and his
ministry are one. This is clearly described when Christ says
that he is always at work, even on the Sabbath (Jn 5:17)

---

[3]Torrance, p. 123.

[4]Here we can even be tempted to say that, if this is true—and I believe it
is—then it is not true to say that ministry is born out of theology. Rather
it seems better to say that theology, as "a word about God," i.e., about his
nature (as far as our limited human minds can go), his economy and his
purpose for his creation, comes forth *from* ministry. Thought about in this
way, theology is a proclamation of God's ministry, and God's ministry is
fully demonstrated in the Incarnation.

and that he must work continuously "while it is day" (Jn 9:4).

Christ's person and his task are one in his role as shepherd. Whenever a person and task are identical it is necessary to use terms which do not limit that person to the function of a "job" or a "profession." This is true in the ministry of the priest; his office and person are the same. Thus, when the scriptural referents to Prophet, King and Priest are made, they give to our understanding of ministry a personal rather than a functional character.[5] Any one of these terms unites within itself the person and his task, the person and his "office." It is necessary to briefly describe the ministry of shepherding in terms of these three aspects since each contributes to the understanding of Christ's role as shepherd of the flock, and in turn, to the contemporary priestly ministry.

The Prophet. The Prophet stands on behalf of God before the people; he "speaks" God's word, leading, challenging, contending. In 1 Kings, Elisha is consecrated by Elijah: "And Elisha . . . you shall anoint to be prophet in your place" (1 Kg 19:16). Psalm 105:15 associates the anointed ones and the prophets: "Touch not my anointed ones and do my prophets no harm!" Both Saul and David are given the prophetic gifts, in which they are anointed "to proclaim the gospel to the poor . . . to preach the acceptable year of the Lord" (Is 61-1 KJV).

---

[5]Although these three roles have often been referred to in various theological studies and sources, especially in the Holy Scripture itself, mostly of which I have used, I am indebted to a wonderful article in *The Scottish Journal of Theology,* Vol. 11, 3, 1958, p. 225 ff. for a most complete analysis, especially in terms of the "priestly" role, i.e., in terms of consecration in the Levitical order of Aaron. I should also like to add that I am not dealing here with the "cosmical" nature of these roles. For example, the "King" was to have dominion over the "cosmos," to care for it as God created him, cf. Genesis; or even as the "Priest" who is to eternally give thanks to God as a "eucharistic being." These are, of course, important, but my intent is to point to the Old Testamental roles as fulfilled in Christ. There certainly is some connection between these approaches, e.g. Adam lost these functions when he "fell," which Christ as the "Second Adam" fulfilled, etc.

In each case, Christ claims to fulfill in himself this prophetic function. We know this, when in St Luke's Gospel, he came into the synagogue at Nazareth on the Sabbath, and stood up to read. Reading from the book of Isaiah, he proclaimed:

> The Spirit of the Lord is upon me, because he has anointed me to preach good news to the poor . . . to proclaim release to the captives . . . to proclaim the acceptable year of the Lord.   (Lk 4:18)

And then, as the eyes of his listeners were "fixed on him," he said: "today this scripture has been fulfilled in your hearing" (Lk 4:21). Later, referring to this prophetic role, he said, "no prophet is acceptable in his own country" (Lk 4:24). Jesus, of course, was in Nazareth, that is, "in his own country."

The prophetic role of Christ's ministry, obviously associated with consecration and anointment, is the service of proclaiming the true wisdom and righteousness of God to the flock. This St Paul writes to the Corinthians: "He is . . . our wisdom, our righteousness and sanctification and redemption" (1 Cor 1:30). All priestly ministry must include this prophetic function, a proclamation (κήρυγμα) as it is "in Christ." The "prophetic" role rightly belongs within the ministry of Christ as shepherd.

The King. The clearest passage regarding the ministry of the Christ as "king" is found in 2 Kings 11:12:

> And they brought forth the King's son, and put the crown upon him, and gave his testimony: and they made him king and anointed him.

Later, the book of Kings speaks of the covenant which is made between "the Lord and the king and people, that they should be the Lord's people" (2 Kg 11:17).

Like the prophet, the king is anointed. David is anointed

three times (cf. 2 Sam 2:4), so that he should receive the gift of the spirit. He is also crowned as a sign of royalty and he lives by a covenant.

Hebrews speaks of the fulfillment of this kingly role in the ministry of Christ:

> But of the Son, he says, "Thy throne, O God, is for ever and ever, the righteous scepter is the scepter of thy kingdom . . . God has anointed thee (Christ) with the oil of gladness." (Heb 1:8-9)

Again, we see in the book of Acts, "how God anointed Jesus of Nazareth with the Holy Spirit and with power; how he went about doing good and healing" (Acts 10:29). And as Christ said of himself in quoting Isaiah: "he has anointed me to preach the good news to the poor" (Lk 4:18). The kingly role, granted through anointment and covenant, is also crucial to the ministry of Christ as shepherd.

The Priest. The third dimension of Christ's ministry as shepherd is the "priestly" *per se*. If the Prophet stands on behalf of God before the people, then the Priest can be best described as standing on behalf of the people before God; he offers life up to God.

Our inquiry into this dimension of Christ's ministry, takes us directly to the liturgical *ordination* and the liturgical *celebration* of the priest. In the Old Testament books of Exodus (28 and 29), Leviticus (6 and 9), and Numbers (8), we find the "priestly prayers" in St John's gospel (chapters 13 to 17).[6] Within Israel, one tribe is set aside for priestly functions, the tribe of Levi (Num 3). Within this tribe of Levi, the "sons of Aaron" are further set aside as special liturgical priests. "It was the business of the Levites and priests (sons of Aaron) to teach the Law to Israel, and so they lived scattered among the twelve tribes."[7]

A very full description of the ordination and consecra-

[6]*Ibid.,* Scottish Journal, p. 26.
[7]*Op. cit.*

tion of priests is given in Exodus 29 and Leviticus 8.[8] When
the entire assembly met at the door of the tabernacle, Aaron
and his sons are brought forth. They are washed at the
Laver and clothed with priestly garments. Only Aaron himself is anointed, being then called *christos,* the anointed one.
His sons are only sprinkled with oil. Then the various sacrifices are offered, some of which are given into the hands
of Aaron and his sons as "fill-offerings," i.e. "their hands
were filled (mille'yadh')."[9] It should be noted here, that
subsequently, whenever each priest died, the eldest son in
the blood line was clothed in his high priestly garments, and
was consecrated in the same way as were the preceding
generations back to Aaron.[10]

Like that of the prophet and the king, the "priestly" role
is central to the proper understanding of the ministry of
Christ as shepherd, and in turn, to a proper understanding
of the shepherd in the contemporary ministry.

In the priestly role—as in each of these roles—a sanctification and consecration by anointment takes place. This involves the oil, covenant, new garments, "filling the hands,"
etc. With Christ, however, something radically new happens, into which the characteristics of this priestly role are
assumed, and by which they are fulfilled. The "order of
Aaron" is abrogated in a new sanctification, and now by
the first and only Christ (*Christos*-anointed one) who completes that order. The "sons of Aaron" as a priestly order

[8] The ordination and consecration rites in the Old Testament are far
more complex than what we are presenting here. Isolated are those parts
that are important to our particular study. I have used in this research two
important sources: Alexander Cruden's *Concordance to the Old and New
Testament* (London: Revell Company, 1953) and the *Jerome Biblical
Commentary,* edited by Raymond Brown, Joseph Fitzmeyer and Roland
Murphy (Englewood, Prentice Hall).

[9] Cf. Ex 29, especially vs 24-28 and footnote in *The New Oxford
Annotated Bible,* RSV (New York: Oxford University Press, 1977). This
literal Hebrew expression—"mille 'yadh' "—denoted investiture with priestly
prerogatives.

[10] Certain of these characteristics, e.g. being clothed with priestly garments, being anointed, and "filling the hands" with that which is sacrificed,
are also found in Baptism (which is an "ordination") and in the Ordination
of the Presbyter (in which the lamb—*amnos*—is given into the hands of the
one ordained, "to protect until the Second Coming").

has finished its mission since it served as a preparation for this new priesthood. The new priesthood is *not* one of progeny and procreation, and the gospel of St John makes this clear.

In John's gospel, we learn through the "high priestly prayer" of Christ, that there is still an anointment, sanctification and consecration, but this time it is *by the Holy Spirit and by the truth of Christ*; in this Christ sanctifies both himself and his disciples.

> Sanctify them in the truth; thy word is truth. As thou didst send me into the world, so I have sent them into the world. And for their sakes I consecrate myself, that they also may be consecrated in truth.
>
> (St John 17:18-19)

In Hebrews, again, we find:

> For he who sanctifies and those who are sanctified have all one origin. That is why he is not ashamed to call them brethren. (Heb. 2:11)

The writer to the Hebrews tells us that there is, in the new High Priest, a change, a new "law"; "For when there is a change in the priesthood, there is necessarily a change in the law as well" (Heb 7:12). The new priesthood is one of eternal life, is "perfect for evermore" (Heb 7:28).

> This becomes even more evident when another priest arises in the likeness of Melchizedek, who has become a priest, not according to a legal requirement concerning bodily descent, but by the power of an indestructible life. (Heb 7:16-16)

The new order, then, which was foretold already in Genesis 14:18, and in Psalm 109:4, is that of Melchizedek, that of an "indestructible life," ordained now by the anointment of the Holy One (1 Jn 2:20 and 27, cf. also 2 Cor 1:21).

He himself is the new High Priest foretold by the prophets, the eternal priest, not according to the order of Aaron, but according to the order of Melchizedek.[11]

With this new law, we see that in Christ's ministry there is a fulfillment of all three roles. However, this fulfillment is not to be understood merely in terms of a similarity in consecration and anointment; Christ fulfills his role as *leitourgos,* the "leader of our worship." That is, he is "a minister of the sanctuary, and the true tent, which is set up not by man but by the Lord" (Heb 8:2). Not only is he that which is offered, but is the offerer as the "minister of the sanctuary."

> But Christ . . . offered himself without blemish to God, a spiritual and eternal sacrifice; and his blood will cleanse our conscience from the deadness of our former ways, and fit us for the service of the living God.   (Heb 9:11-15, see also 10:1-25 NEB)

As the "minister of the sanctuary," Christ is the sole Priest, the sole celebrant. All those who, after Christ, serve as a "minister of the sanctuary," make him present; they are presenting *him who is there.* In this sense, Georges Florovsky speaks of the celebrants of liturgical ministry not as a group of "officers" who are acting *in persona ecclesiae.* Instead:

> they are acting primarily *in persona Christi.* They are representatives of Christ himself, not of believers; and in them and through them the Head of the Body, the only High Priest of the New Covenant, is performing, continuing and accomplishing his eternal pastoral and priestly office. He is himself the only true minister of the Church.[12]

[11]Wilhelm Stockhums, *The Priesthood* (Rockford, Illinois: Tan Publishers, Inc., 1974, p. 5).
[12]*Ibid.,* Florovsky, p. 65.

This means for us today, that the shepherd, when he is celebrating as priest, does nothing by himself; this is only how we can use the word "represent," that is, that he re-*presents* Christ; he is "presenting" Christ who is always there.

This does not mean, however, that the shepherd as celebrating priest today, has no part in the liturgical sacrifice, but only that it is now in the "one true minister of the Church" that his function can be realized; indeed, this ministry is *delivered* to the celebrating priest by the truly present High Priest. This is captured in the Eucharistic Divine Liturgy:

> ... and as Ruler of all didst become our High Priest, and didst deliver unto us the ministry of this liturgical and bloodless sacrifice ... (the Prayer of the Cherubic Hymn of the Liturgy)

And as a response to this ministry committed to us by Christ (who is now present even with "thousands of arch-angels, and hosts of angels, the Cherubim and the Seraphim"), the celebrating priest in that Liturgy can only be thankful on behalf of the entire people:

> ... and we give thanks unto thee also for this ministry (ὑπὲρ τῆς λειτουργίας ταύτης) which thou did vouchsafe *to receive* at our hands ... (The Anaphora of the Liturgy of St John Chrysostom)

However, although this ministry has been, at once, "delivered" by Christ to the celebrating priest, and "re-ceived" by Christ from the celebrating priest ("thou didst vouchsafe to receive at our hands"), it is in no way something which that celebrating priest himself is able or worthy to accomplish; it is only because Christ who is truly present, is pouring out his mercies and bounties:

> Wherefore, O all-holy Master, we also, thy sinful and unworthy servants, whom thou hast graciously *permitted to minister* (λειτουργεῖν) at thy Holy Altar, not through our own righteousness (for we

have done no good deed upon the earth), but because
of thy *mercies and bounties, which thou hast richly
poured out upon us,* have now boldness to draw
near. . . .   (Anaphora of St Basil's Liturgy)

But despite the celebrating priest's participation in
Christ's own ministry, there must be no mistake: it is always
and only Christ who is the *leitourgos,* the "leader of our
worship," the one true "mediator." This St Paul writes to
Timothy, in which he exhorts that "supplications, prayers,
intercessions and thanksgiving be made for all men," but
then goes on to add:

For there is one God, and there is one mediator
between God and men, the man Christ Jesus, who
gave himself as a ransom for all.   (1 Tim 2:1-6)

How is it that Christ is the only true mediator? The only
true celebrant? Where are the roots of this understanding?
This role of *leitourgos,* again, is connected with the Old
Testamental priesthood. The Day of Atonement was the
one day in which an offering was made to God, which
"gathered up" all the other offerings made daily in the
sanctuary.[13] On that day, the worship of all Israel was led
by one man, the high priest. He was the representative of all
Israel, standing in solidarity with them. To show this solidarity, on his breastplace were inscribed the names of all
twelve tribes of Israel. At that time, he confessed the sins
of the people over the head of the sacrificial lamb, and in
the name of the people, entered the Holy of Holies. There
he interceded with God for the people, and returning to the
people, pronounced the Aaronic blessing of peace.
What is important in this is that, first, when the high
priest entered into the Holy of Holies, all Israel entered in
the person of that high priest, and secondly, when he entered
within the veil with the blood of the lamb, God accepted
all of Israel.

[13]This information regarding the offering on the Day of Atonement can
be found in the *Church Service Society Annual,* No. 40, May 1970,
pp.41-62 by James B. Torrance, "The Place of Jesus Christ in Worship."

The obvious connection is made in terms of Christ as the new high priest who is *leitourgos,* in that when he enters the sanctuary "not made with hands" (Heb 9:11), we are entered *with* him. Furthermore, it is his own blood which is shed, and by which we are accepted. Hebrews, again, captures this point:

> But when Christ appeared as a high priest . . . through the greater and more perfect tent (not made by hands, that is, not of this creation) he entered once for all into the Holy Place, taking not the blood of goats and calves, but his own blood, thus securing an eternal redemption. (Heb 9:11-12)

For those who serve in this ministry "according to the order of Melchizedek," who follow in "representing" the one true *leitourgos,* we now have the same boldness to enter with him: "Therefore, brethren, . . . we have confidence to enter the sanctuary by the blood of Jesus" (Heb 10:18).

4. Christ's Ministry and the Father

In considering both Christ's eternal priesthood and now his liturgical ministry, it has been noted that his role as shepherd is related to what he is. But his ministry (as service) is also, and always, *humble*; it is always in relationship to the One who sent him, that is, the Father.[14] When Jesus Christ acts, it is God the Father who acts, and who is revealed in that act. "I can do nothing on my own authority; . . .

[14]We will not deal here with the relationship of Christ and the Holy Spirit, nor with the crucial role of the Spirit in the ministry; that will come later. Obviously, ordination itself is accomplished through the Spirit, and obviously, the mystery of Pentecost must be considered. For our present purposes, however, we are concerned with the meaning of Christ's relationship with the Father, and with the community having its identity as Christ's Body. Father Florovsky says what we mean here: "The Church as a whole, has her personal center only in Christ, she is not an incarnation of the Holy Spirit, nor is she merely a Spirit-bearing community, but precisely the Body of Christ, the Incarnate Lord" ("The Church: Her Nature and Task," Ibid., vol. 1, p. 67).

I seek not my own will, but the will of him who sent me" (Jn 5:30) are the words of Christ himself. These follow the declaration that "as the Father has life in himself, so he has granted the Son also to have life in himself" (Jn 5:26). He therefore is the Son of this Father, and his ministry is reflected as one of humility before the Father: "the Father is greater than I" (Jn 14:28); he has not come of himself, but the Father has sent him (Jn 8:42). And even if it seems that he "honors" himself, that is "nothing" in light of this humility before the Father:

> If I glorify myself, my glory is nothing; it is my Father who glorifies me, of whom you say that he is your God.   (Jn 8:54)

Because this oneness between Christ and the Father is present, St John's gospel tells us that he speaks what he has heard from the Father (8:26). What the Father has commanded him, he does (14:31). He does what "pleases" the Father (8:29). He declares the "name" of the Father in which he speaks (17:26). All this means that Christ's ministry is the Father's ministry, the Father working through Christ (114:10). Finally, however, we receive the ultimate word regarding this: "I and the Father are one" (Jn 10:30). Thus, in terms of ministry, "He who believes in me, believes not in me, but in him who sent me" (Jn 12:44). It is this which Christ makes clear to Philip, who not yet understanding these words, seeks to "see" the Father:

> Philip said to him, "Lord show us the Father, and we will be satisfied." Jesus said to him, "Have I been with you so long, and you yet do not know me? He who has seen me has seen the Father, Philip."
>   (Jn 14:9)

If it is true, then, that Christ and the Father are one, we can even say, in this sense, that the ministry of Christ begins from before his appearance in Galilee, i.e. even before the Incarnation. "Before Abraham was, I am" (Jn

8:57). There was no such "conversion" of Christ (an ancient heresy) in which his ministry begins, even if the fullness of his ministry on earth is revealed in the Incarnation. He is "from the foundation of the world" with the Father, i.e. before his fleshly appearance.

We find a clue to this when Jesus is but the twelve year old boy who is found "sitting among the teachers, listening to them and asking them questions" (Lk 2:46). We find there that he must already "be about his Father's business" (Lk 2:49, KJV); this is what his parents could not understand (Lk 2:50). This eternal ministry is also known by St John the Forerunner in the Jordan; the Baptist recognized Christ before the baptism (Mt 3:14) for which reason he did not deem himself worthy to baptize him.

Thus Christ's ministry, since it is one with his life (which is eternal), is before the world and exists beyond the world. Being one with the Father, his ministry is eternal, and those who minister in this temporal world, also participate in his eternal ministry.

Because Christ's ministry is eternal we are reminded of just how radically new is this priesthood. Despite all which has been presented, we cannot be satisfied in observing it merely as some "continuation" of the Old Testamental priesthood; Christ does not come merely to "modify" the Aaronic priesthood. Indeed, if the words "fulfill" and "new" can be used, these words are meant in this radical sense: Christ "fills up" (fulfills) the existing form, the external appearance, and the function of the Old Testament priesthood, with *new* content and meaning; this priesthood comes from without and not from within; it is not a new link in an evolutionary chain. His priesthood, the core of his ministry, although it has made its appearance in the world of humans, is nevertheless born from the world of God, i.e. precisely as an eternal ministry, precisely "out of this world." The form may indeed have been continuous, but the content of this ministry is purely God's content: it is outside human lines, and human time and space, even if God uses those forms to prepare for this priesthood.

If there is an ancient "tree of the priesthood" (of

Aaron), the new priesthood comes into it *ad extra,* and has not grown out of it. The confrontation of our Lord with the last high priest Caiphas clearly exemplifies this radically new priesthood. Wilhelm Stockums vividly describes the moment of change:

> When the high priest Caiphas, at the trial of Jesus before the Sanhedrin, solemnly *tore his garment,* he performed an action that, without his own intent or knowledge, symbolized the destruction of the Old Testamental priesthood. The last high priest of the Old Law was judicially retired from office in precisely that moment when the new High Priest in the person of Christ, stood before him ... the former (Caiphas) lending him unwitting but most effective assistance by imposing the death sentence.[15]

Thus, the eternal moment is realized when these two high priests confront each other, the one to bury forever his priestly power, the other to inaugurate the new and eternal priesthood.

From all that has been said regarding the ministry of Christ as "shepherd," it can be concluded that the priest as shepherd today, being *in persona Christi,* is indeed the "servant," as is Christ. However, it cannot be forgotten that his action, in its essence, is itself an *actio Christi*; he does not say "This is the body of Christ, this is the blood of Christ ..."; he does say "This is My Body, this is My Blood." That Christ himself is made present, and that we are servants *in* that presence, St John Chrysostom says:

> The words set before us are not of man's power. He that then did these things at that supper, this same one now also works. We occupy the place of servants. He who sanctifieth and changeth them is the same.[16]

Christ as the sole Priest is the *causa efficiens principalis,*

[15]*Ibid.,* Stockums, p. 13.
[16]*Homily 82* on St Matthew 26:26-28 (P.G. LVIII, p. 744).

i.e. the efficient cause from whom and in whom our ministry is possible; as a response, the priests's ministry is *causa instrumentalis,* the instrument in the hands of Christ. Christ is the cause, we are the response.

From this meaning of Christ's ministry as the shepherd, we can move on to what is involved on the part of those "shepherds" who place themselves, as active servants, into the hands of Christ. We move to the apostolic ministry.

CHAPTER TWO

The First Shepherds after Christ

"As the Father has sent me, even so I send you" (Jn 20:21). These are the words by which Christ's ministry as shepherd is is extended to his disciples and apostles.

Christ extends his ministry to these specially chosen few in a striking manner. St Luke and St Mark relate how the Lord advanced this ministry of leadership to them. After passing the night in prayer on the mountain top, St Luke says, "And when it was day, he called his disciples, and chose from them twelve, whom he named apostles" (6:13). St Mark lays special emphasis on the uniqueness of this call: "And he appointed twelve, to be with him" (3:14). Obviously, we learn from this special choosing, that not everyone is to minister as a shepherd (although certainly every Christian is to minister in some form within the community, according to God's gifts).

1. Characteristics of Christ's Shepherds

There are certain characteristics of these apostles and disciples which are required in their ministry as shepherds. In the New Testament we find several—although certainly not all—of these qualifying characteristics, which also are clearly extended to the contemporary ministry. There are three such characteristics which are fundamental, and which we shall briefly describe.

Homo Dei. The apostle of Christ must be an example

of the "man of God," as St Paul says to Timothy: "Set the believers an example in speech and conduct, in love, in faith, in purity" (1 Tim 4:12). Any Christian today, by the same extension of Christ's ministry, must also be such an example. This title, "man of God," is directly given by St Paul, warning that one must, first of all, flee from those certain things which can "entangle" him and keep him from focusing upon God.

> For the love of money is the root of all evils; it is through this craving that some have wandered away from the faith and pierced their hearts with many pangs. But as for you, man of God, shun all this.
>   (1 Tim 6:10)

The apostle and disciple, thus, is not only *of* and *in* Christ, but also *for* Christ; his entire life is to be aimed, not toward anything else in this world, but only toward God:

> Do not be conformed to this world but be transformed by the renewal of your mind, that you may prove what is the will of God, what is good and acceptable and perfect.   (Rom 12:2)

It is only by "putting off" this world (while acting responsibility in it) that the pastor of today "puts on" the ministry of the New Man: "put on the new nature, created after the likeness of God in true righteousness and holiness" (Eph 4:23ff). St Paul says this *homo Dei* must also pursue, and even "fight" for, his ministry:

> Aim at righteousness, godliness, faith, love, steadfastness, gentleness. Fight the good fight of faith; take hold of the eternal life, to which you were called.
>   (1 Tim 6:11)

When St Peter writes to the "Elders" he further reminds them as men of God, that they are to be "types" or "patterns" (τύποι) to the flocks which they shepherd.

Tend the flock of God that is your charge, not by constraint but willingly... eagerly, not as domineering over those in your charge, but being examples (τύποι) to the flock. (1 Pet 5:2-3)

This, St Peter goes on to say, is the way each of us, particularly the shepherd of today, will receive his "crown" from the Chief Shepherd.

And when the Chief Shepherd is manifested, you will obtain the unfading crown of glory. (1 Pet 5:2-3)

Finally, when St Paul writes to Titus, who is called to be one such *homo Dei,* it is always that he should serve as such an example:

Show yourself in all respects as a model of good deeds, and in your teaching show integrity, gravity, and sound speech. (Tit 2:7ff)

Although the patristic sources on the ministry will be dealt with later, we can turn to one who directly addresses this task for the pastor of today. It is St Gregory the Great of Rome who seems to have taken the call for this *homo Dei* as a central focus in his *Pastoral Rule.* In this example he summarizes for us this first characteristic of the disciple and apostle as *homo Dei.*

That man, therefore, ought by all means to be drawn with cords to be an example of good living, who already lives spiritually, dying to all passions of the flesh; ... who desires only inward wealth ... who gives freely of himself, not wanting things that belong to others ... who is quick to pardon, but never bent down to pardon more than is proper ... who perpetuates no unlawful deeds, yet deplores those perpetuated by others as if they were his own ... who sympathizes with another's infirmities, and also rejoices in the good of his neighbor as though it were his own.
                    (Reg. Past. I, cap, 10, PL.LXXVII, 23)

Sal Terrae, Lux Mundi. "You are the salt of the earth . . . you are the light of the world" (Mt 5:13-14). These are metaphors, spoken of together, which Christ calls his apostles in his Sermon on the Mount, and they clearly apply to the contemporary ministry. *Salt* both preserves and gives season to the food: this the primitive people to whom he spoke could well understand, since salt was imperative to their daily life. In terms of ministry, the apostles are reminded that they are to live according to this imagery, in order to preserve both themselves and those who follow them from decay. In a like manner, their words and example as shepherds are to give season, i.e. potency and savor, to the potential faith of the people. But there is a warning to these shepherds:

> If salt has lost its taste, how shall its saltness be restored? It is no longer good for anything except to be thrown out and trodden under foot by men.
>
> (Mt 5:13)

Like the salt, the *light* is also a characteristic which our Lord claims belongs to their ministry. They are serving as the light of the revelation, i.e. to reveal the one who spoke of himself: "I am the light of the world" (Jn 8:12). The primitive people, again knowing the value of the light for their lives (especially in their age), could well understand the importance of this metaphor in terms of ministry. Light is truth (since they both have to do with a proper seeing), and since Christ is the truth about all existence, their light was to reveal this Truth: "For this I was born, and for this I have come into the world, to bear witness to the truth" (Jn 18:37). Again, Christ came to "enlighten every man that comes into the world" (Jn 1:9). Thus, the ministry of the apostles, like that of today, is to be shepherds who lead by this "light."

Bonus miles. "Share in suffering as a good soldier of Christ Jesus. No soldier in service gets entangled in civilian pursuits, since his aim is to satisfy the one who enlisted him" (2 Tim 2:3). The apostolic ministry could well be thought of as a warfare, with the shepherd as a *soldier*. The enemy of this soldier is both from without and from within, e.g. sin, error, evil, unbelief, etc. This characteristic of the good soldier is made very graphic by St Paul:

> Therefore take the whole armor of God, that you may be able to withstand in the evil day, and having done all, to stand. Stand therefore . . . having put on the breastplate of righteousness . . . taking the shield of faith . . . the helmet of salvation . . . the sword of the Spirit, which is the word of God.   (Eph 6:13-17)

This "military" language which characterizes the apostolic ministry as that of the good soldier, does not come to St Paul lightly; his ministry, which can be autobiographically seen in 2 Corinthians (11:23-33) shows that he suffered through many battles and sufferings for the sake of Christ. Thus he can say, when his days as a shepherd are at their end: "I have fought the good fight" (2 Tim 4:7).

For those shepherds today, i.e., the pastors who are the "leaders" in the ministry of Christ, the "good soldier" imagery is no less relevant. Their ministry, in this sense, is as Christ declared in the presence of his apostles: "Do not think that I came to bring peace on earth: I have not come to bring peace, but a sword" (Mt 10:34). The "sword" which he sends, is the sword not of bloody battles, but the sword of the Spirit, one which cleaves and discerns between truth and falsehood, good and evil, God and the devil.

Such a shepherd of today, then, cannot minister in the Body unless he also can be described by such characteristics as these: a man of God, the salt, the light, the soldier, etc. "This is how one should regard us, as servants of Christ and stewards of the mysteries of God" (1 Cor 4:1). These, of course, are merely descriptive terms; there are many more, e.g. "ambassadors" (2 Cor 5:20), and as was mentioned, each could well apply to *all* Christians in their ministry.

2. The Twelve and the Seventy

Seeing what qualities were to be present for those who were the first shepherds after Christ, i.e. in the apostolic ministry, still does not explain how their *role and function* as shepherds actually came about and developed in the community. Consequently, we must now explain the *genesis and development* of the ministry as it followed that of the Great Shepherd. According to scripture, the ministry of these shepherds seems to develop in three stages, in relation to three groups of ministers: The Twelve Apostles, The Seventy Disciples, and the *Episkopoi-Presbyteroi* (Overseers-Pastors).

It must first be stated that, before the development of the triadic ministry of the clergy (bishop, presbyter/priest, deacon), there seems to be a pluralism in terms of "titles" of ministry in the New Testament.[1] The "offices" as we know them today, were not fixed. For example, "at Corinth there was a loosely structured community guided by St Paul in which each had his special gift for service of the community" (1 Cor 12:8ff).[2] Similarly, at Philippi the leaders were called *episkopoi* and *diakonoi*. At Thessalonica the leaders were simply those who "are over you in the Lord" (1 Th 5:12). And at Ephesus, there were "pastor-teachers" (Eph 4:11). Obviously, there was some fluidity in both function and title, especially between the *episcopos* and *presbyteros* which were only later fully developed as "offices" by the fourth century.[3] But whatever the "titles," a scheme of ministry within the scripture can be seen in these early years, and this scheme has implications for the ministry today.

"Already at the beginning of the public ministry we have seen how the Lord called to him the twelve; these apostles were evidently the pastors and doctors of the Church that

---

[1]Edward Echlin, *The Priest as Preacher* (Fides Publishers, Notre Dame, Inc.) p. 23. This is part of a series entitled *Theoolgy Today*, No. 33. No date is given.

[2]*Op. cit.*, this source also for the diversity of titles which follow.

[3]*Ibid.*, p. 24. Father Echlin is making his point that many titles and thus, many functions, were not as yet distinct. His claim is that this triadic formation was not fully developed until at least the fourth century.

Jesus intended to found. They will always remain as such."[4]
But there is to be seen here, at once, a distinction and a connection between the *specific* ministry of the twelve apostles
and the more *general* ministry of Christ's seventy disciples.[5]

After Judas falls away, it is Matthias who will replace
him. What is interesting, however, is Peter's response when
the question arises as to this replacement. He should be
chosen from:

> One of the men who have accompanied us during
> all the time that the Lord Jesus went in and out
> among us, beginning from the baptism of John until
> the day when he was taken up from us. (Acts 1:21-22)

This tells us, obviously, that there was a group of faithful disciples, in fact seventy, who followed Christ closely,
like the twelve apostles themselves.[6] That such disciples are
distinct from the twelve, can be seen in various examples,
e.g. when persons are given certain requirements to "test"
them, if they want to "follow him" (Lk 9:57-62 and
18:18:30, Mt 8:19-22 and 19:16-30, and Mk 10:17-31). The
existence of these disciples already tells us that there is a
"general" ministry which we can say today is given at
baptism, i.e. the *ministry of the laity,* and which, by way of
analogy (although in no absolute manner), is distinct from
the ministry of the *clergy.* (This will be dealt with shortly.)[7]
This general ministry of his disciples, distinct from the twelve
(as a "specific" ministry analogous to the clergy), can be
summarized in two statements, both of which point to the
requirement that the ultimate desire of these seventy before
all else (family, job, home, burying the dead, wife, etc.),

[4]Lebreton and Zeiller, *The Church in the New Testament* (New York:
Collier Books, 1962) p. 127.

[5]St Luke's language leads us to believe that Jesus called the apostles
from *among* the disciples. (Luke 6:13) However, the commemoration of
these two groups is always found in the Preparation of the Holy Oblations
(Proskomedia) at the Eucharist Liturgy; the celebrant always remembers
"The Twelve and the Seventy."

[6]*Ibid.,* Lebreton and Zeiller, p. 128.

[7]We in no way are proposing that this general ministry could not be

is a *commitment* to the Kingdom of God in which one cannot "look back." This, of course, is always set in the dynamic of abandonment of slavery to earthly goods:

> No one who puts his hand to the plow and looks back, is fit for the Kingdom of God.   (Lk 9:62)

And,

> If thou will be perfect, go sell what thou hast and give to the poor, and thou shall have treasure in heaven: and come and follow me.   (Lk 18:22 KJV)

But these disciples, beyond the twelve, are called not only to follow him with such commitment; they are also sent by Him to *minister.* Lebreton and Zeiller remind us that they were seventy (70) in number and that their ministry was generally to those in southern Palestine. "At the beginning of the journeys in which Jesus was once more to undertake the evangelization of southern Palestine, he sent forth seventy disciples on a mission."[8]

We find the exact challenge of the ministry of these seventy in St Luke:

> After this, the Lord appointed seventy others and sent them on ahead of him, two by two, into every town and place where he himself was about to come. And he said to them. . . . Go your way; behold, I send you out as lambs in the midst of wolves. Carry no purse, no bag, no sandals; and salute no one on the road. Whatever house you enter, first say, "Peace be to this house!" And if a son of peace is there, your peace shall rest upon him; but if not, it shall return to you. And remain in the same house, eating and

a precedent for either the clergy or the laity today; we mean this only analogically, and as an *entry* to discuss the general ministry of all Christians in the Body, which is to follow in our discussion.

[8]*Ibid.,* p. 130 The authors inform their readers that there are two accounts: one says seventy, the other seventy-two. The difference, they claim, is unimportant.

drinking what they provide, for the laborer deserves
his wages. (Lk 10:1-7)

If the ministry of the twelve apostles seemed to be that
of the leaders of the Apostolic Church centered around the
area of Galilee, then it was the seventy disciples who extended this ministry to the larger area of the southern
provinces.[9] It is interesting that when these seventy disciples
return from their ministry, it is with great joy in having
won a victory over Satan and for the name of Jesus Christ.
The Lord and his disciples are filled with this joy:

> The seventy returned with joy, saying, "Lord, even
> the demons are subject to us in your name!" And
> he said to them, "I saw Satan fall like lightning from
> heaven." (Lk 10:17-18)

This rejoicing of the Lord at seeing the victory of their
ministry for the Kingdom, i.e. at seeing "Satan fall," is followed by a beautiful prayer of thanksgiving; joy such as
this can only be followed by thanksgiving.

> In that same hour [Jesus] rejoiced in the Holy Spirit
> and said, "I thank thee, Father, Lord of heaven and
> earth, that thou hast hidden these things from the
> wise and understanding, and revealed them to babes;
> yea, Father, for such was thy gracious will.
> (Lk 10:21-22)

This prayer of thanksgiving for their ministry in his
name and for the Kingdom, is followed immediately by an
explanation to the seventy of what actually has been given
to them:

> Then turning to the disciples he said privately,
> "Blessed are the eyes which see what you see! For
> I tell you, that many prophets and kings desired to

[9]*Op. cit.*

see what you see, and did not see it, and to hear
what you hear, and did not hear it." (Lk 10:24)

The gift of ministry which the seventy disciples received
points to the extension of ministry beyond that of the close
group of the twelve disciples.

But obviously the ministry of the twelve apostles is a
"special" ministry. These apostles, chosen from among the
disciples, were to "sit on thrones judging the twelve tribes
of Israel" (Lk 22:30). "The idea of 'the twelve' is not
merely a post-resurrection development. For the twelve disciples, because they were with Jesus from the beginning of
his public ministry, are unique."[10] Standing over the twelve
tribes of Israel, the twelve are the eschatological sign of the
New Jerusalem, i.e. "in the resurrection" (Mt 22:28). Thus
the focus of their ministry as leaders and shepherds, which
sets the standard for those shepherds (clergy) that followed, rests in the proclamation of the resurrection of Christ
of which they were direct witnesses. This is seen in St Peter's
sermon at Jerusalem: "This Jesus God raised up, of that we
all are witnesses" (Acts 2:32).

That they were direct witnesses, and that the uniqueness
of their ministry at Jerusalem was thus focused, can be seen
in their obstinacy before the Jewish authorities:

And the high priest questioned them saying, "We
strictly charged you not to teach in this name [of
Jesus], yet here you have filled Jerusalem with your
teaching and you intend to bring this man's blood
upon us." (Acts 5:27-28)

It was Peter and the other apostles who, having now received the Holy Spirit, could answer: "We must obey God
rather than men" (Acts 5:29). The courage to answer in
this manner could only be because "we are witnesses to
these things and so is the Holy Spirit whom God has given
to those who obey him" (Acts 5:32).

What follows seems to be the very first persecution of

[10]*Ibid.*, Echlin, p. 12.

Christians, mostly led by the Sadducees.[11] These Sadducees (who said there was no resurrection), unlike the scribes and Pharisees, had hoped that their particular problems would end with the death of Jesus. Yet, it was this ministry which would not allow Christ's own ministry to die.

It is interesting also that the accusations and persecution which followed the forbiddance that these twelve should thus preach, was not founded on the Sabbath and the Law (which the Pharisees held against Christ). Rather it was that they should not minister "in his name" (Acts 4:7ff). Yet, it was precisely "in his name" that they did minister as the leaders of the Church, healing and preaching. "Now many signs and wonders were done among the people by the hands of the apostles" (Acts 5:12).

This ministry "in his name" infuriated the Sanhedrin, who wanted the apostles put to death: "When they heard this they were enraged and wanted to kill them" (Acts 5:33). It was on the urging of the physician Gamaliel (who, ironically, was a Pharisee) that they were not killed. They were, however, scourged and beaten, after which they were again warned not to minister and preach "in his name."

The apostles, however, left these tortures "rejoicing that they were counted worthy to suffer dishonor for the name" (Acts 5:41). In fact, "every day in the temple and at home they did not cease teaching and preaching Jesus as the Christ" (Acts 5:42).

These twelve, then, who were direct witnesses, shepherded the early community with assurance and joy, despite the fact that they were "uneducated, common men" (Acts 4:13). This was only the beginning of the persecution which would tread upon all those who ministered "in his name." Their ministry could be summarized as follows:

> These first conflicts were but a foretaste of the per-
> secution which was soon to break out; but already
> we perceive in the Apostles the power of the Holy
> Spirit promised by Jesus a little while before; the

[11]*Ibid.*, p. 174, Lebreton and Zeiller, claim that the Scribes and Pharisees did not interfere here, as they did with Jesus.

priests were surprised to find such assurance in un-
lettered men whom they thought they could easily
intimidate; after the scourging it was still more as-
tonishing to find such joy in men so recently weak.[12]

The twelve, then, being direct "witnesses," courageously
serve as the prototype for all shepherds (clergy) which followed them. It soon became apparent, however, that if these
twelve were to properly continue their "shepherding" of the
community, their ministry would have to be extended not
only through the ministry of the seventy but through yet
another new function: the *diaconal* ministry.

These deacons, like the seventy, were not, as such, "shepherds," i.e. leaders of the flock, but clearly their role began
as a direct extension of the early shepherding role of the
Twelve, now expressed through a special function. This new
division in function came about because of a crisis between
the Hellenists and the Hebrews; the Hellenists claimed that
"their widows were neglected in the daily distribution"
(Acts 6:1). "According to Luke, the twelve considered their
own prayerful ministry of the word so important, that they
declined to engage in this social work."[13]

To accomplish the immediate needs of this ministry to
the Hellenists, those who were chosen all bore Greek names:
Stephen, Philip, Prochorus, Nicanor, Timon, Parmenas and
Nicholas (Acts 6:5). As the twelve summoned together
the entire body of disciples, they explained the reason for
this ministry:

It is not right that we should give up preaching the
word of God to serve tables. Therefore, brethren, pick
from among you seven men of good repute, full of
the Spirit and of wisdom, whom we may appoint to
this duty. But we will devote ourselves to prayer and
to the ministry of the word.   (Acts 6:2-3)

This does not mean, however, that these diaconal min-

[12]*Ibid.,* p. 175.
[13]*Ibid.,* Echlin, p. 13.

isters did nothing but "serve tables"; Stephen and Philip are
both found preaching and teaching also, as can be seen
in chapters 6 through 8 of Acts. What is to be noted, however, is that this particular ministry (literally as "servers")
is held as one of great importance; this can be seen in the
ordination which they received. After the "whole multitude"
chose the seven,

> These they set [presented] before the apostles and
> they prayed and laid their hands upon them.
>
> (Acts 6:7)

The diaconal ministry seems to give new impulse to the
community, since soon:

> The word of God increased; and the number of the
> disciples multiplied greatly in Jerusalem and a great
> many of the priests were obedient to the faith.
>
> (Acts 6:7)

From this brief overview, then, it can be seen that this
special ministry of the diaconate served as a crucial function in the Apostolic era, although basically as an expansion
of the ministry of the twelve.[14] Although they were not
"shepherds," the ministry of Christ was expanded both
through their "service" of ministering to the "widows" and
through their evangelizing. (Note here, St Stephen's preaching on the "history of salvation," for which he was martyred
in the presence of Paul, as well as St Philip's explanation of
Isaiah—and thus, of salvation through Christ—to the Ethiopian eunuch on the Gaza road, whom he later baptized.)

---

[14]There is much more that could be said then regarding the diaconate,
e.g. deaconesses and their distinct "ministry," but this is not a study of the
diaconate; we wish to show merely its relationship to the shepherding
(leading) function of the Twelve, and then, only in the Apostolic era.

3. Pastors of Churches: Timothy, Titus and The Elders

In the beginning of the Pastoral Epistles addressed to Timothy and Titus, St Paul states that he sent them to *abide* in Ephesus and Crete, respectively, that, in these locations, they might "amend what was defective, and appoint and ordain elders . . . and give instruction in sound doctrine" (Ti 1:5, 9). From this, one gets a first glimpse of the *residential* aspect of the apostolic ministry, which closely resembles the role of both the bishop and priest in the contemporary ministry. These apostles are sent by Paul to *reside* in the local church, and are to *ordain* others.[15] Thus, they are the third and final stage in the expansion of the apostolic ministry: The Twelve (with the diaconate who are not shepherds), the Seventy sent by our Lord, and now, the pastors (*presbyteroi*) and overseers (*episcopoi*) of the Church sent by the Apostle Paul.[16]

The ministry of these shepherds in the late first century was to preserve the faith:

Follow the pattern of the sound words which you have heard from me, in faith and love which are in Christ Jesus; guard the truth that has been entrusted to you by the Holy Spirit who dwells within us.

(2 Tim 1:13-14)

But to preserve means to continue the tradition of the apostles, maintaining sound doctrine,

Continue in what you have learned and have firmly believed, knowing from whom you learned it.

(2 Tim 3:14)

---

[15]Cf. W. H. Griffith Thomas' *Ministerial Life and Work* (Grand Rapids: Baker Book House, 1978) Chapter III and IV "The Ministry of St Paul" and "The Ministry in the Pastoral Epistles."

[16]For purposes of our study solely on the ministry, and in this chapter, on the shepherding aspect (leading), we mean by "apostolic," those factors

And,

> Teach what befits sound doctrine.   (Ti 2:1)

What seems to mark this "residential" ministry, is the effort both to preserve and continue (deliver) the truth of the gospel in gentleness and charity; this, of course, remains as a central task in the contemporary ministry of the shepherd.

> And the Lord's servant must not be quarrelsome but kindly to every one, an apt teacher, forbearing, correcting his opponents with gentleness. (2 Tim 2:24)

They are to hold fast to what they have received from Paul, but always in the faith and love of Jesus Christ (2 Tim 1:13). Indeed, to be at once firm and gentle is a tension that was not, and never will be, an easy task in the ministry of the shepherd. However, encouraged by St Paul, they are to be "unfailing" in ministering within this tension:

> Preach the word, be urgent in season and out of season, convince, rebuke and exhort, be unfailing in patience and in teaching.   (2 Tim 4:2)

And,

> Declare these things; exhort, and reprove with all authority. Let no one disregard you.   (Ti 2:15)

Although Paul tells Timothy and Titus to be "unfailing" shepherds, he also clearly warns that those to whom they are sent, may not accept them. Can this be any different for shepherds in the contemporary ministry?

By so doing, these pastors will be able to "set the believers an example in speech and conduct, in love, in faith, in purity" (1 Tim 4:12).

regarding the ministry as are found in the Scripture itself. The following portions will deal with later developments of the ministry, e.g. patristic interpretation, etc.

It is out of the faithfulness of such shepherds (at this third stage of development) that others were soon to be ordained in a like capacity; the torch of their ministry was to be passed on to other pastors of the churches.

> What you have heard from me before many witnesses entrust to faithful men who will be able to teach others also.   (2 Tim 2:2)

Paul adds, however,

> Do not be hasty in the laying on of hands!
>   (1 Tim 5:22)

Timothy and Titus are made aware of certain qualifications for the establishment of other elders as residential shepherds. "If any one aspires to the office of bishop (*episcopos*), he desires a noble task ... [but] a bishop must be above reproach" (1 Tim 3:1 ff).

Formally, however, St Paul says to Timothy:

> Let the elders who rule well be considered worthy of double honor, especially those who labor in preaching and teaching; for the scripture says, "You shall not muzzle an ox when it is treading out the grain," and, "The laborer deserves his wages."   (1 Tim 5:17-18)

It is when the pastors of churches are established, that the apostolic ministry (in terms of its scriptural genesis and development) comes to a close. But this is only the beginning of the development of the Church's ministry of the shepherd. The current triadic ministry of clergy leadership: bishop, priest (presbyter) and deacon, begins to take shape as early as the first century.

4. The Holy Spirit in Ministry

In studying the action of the Holy Spirit in ministry, we

are taken beyond the specific role of the shepherd. That
is to say, the "gifts," the *charismata* of the Holy Spirit, are
bestowed in both dimensions of the ministry: in the ministry of the shepherd as "leader," as indicated by the "laying on of hands" to the clergy (*cleros*), and in the ministry
of the laity (*laos*) as received in baptism.

The intent here, however, is not to investigate the important doctrinal teachings regarding the Holy Spirit as
such, but only the relationship of the Spirit to the ministry,
and especially to the ministry of *all* believers (clergy
and laity).[17]

Of Clergy. "For the Holy Spirit takes what is Christ's
and declares it to men, bringing to remembrance all that
Jesus has said and done, guiding men into all truth."[18] In
this statement, Thomas Hopko has captured the activity of
the Holy Spirit in relation to the ministry. The Holy Spirit
declares, brings to remembrance, and guides all that is
Christ's own ministry, as it can now be activated in those
shepherds who minister in him and after him, i.e. the ministry of the clergy.

Such activity of the Spirit in relationship to this "special"
ministry is most clearly expressed at Pentecost.

> When the day of Pentecost had come, they were all
> together in one place. And suddenly a sound came
> from heaven like the rush of a mighty wind, and it
> filled all the house. And there appeared to them
> tongues as of fire distributed and resting on each
> one of them. And they were all filled with the Holy
> Spirit.   (Acts 2:1-4)

This outpouring of the Holy Spirit is promised by Jesus

---

[17]For an excellent study on the action of the Holy Spirit, these terms,
which are beyond our particular focus, see *The Spirit of God* by Thomas
Hopko (Wilton, Conn.: Morehouse Barlow Company, Inc.) 1976. I have
also found, in a more concise manner, an excellent chapter in the book
God and Charity, entitled "God and Man in the Orthodox Church" by the
same author, which can serve a similar function (Brookline, Mass.: Holy
Cross Orthodox Press, 1979) pp. 1-31.

[18]*Ibid.,* Thomas Hopko, in *God and Charity,* p. 12.

to all those who minister "in his name." It was only now that Jesus had "gone away from them" (Jn 16:7) that the Spirit (παράκλητος) would come.

> It is expedient for you that I go away: for if I go not away, the Comforter will not come upon you; but if I depart, I will send him unto you.   (Jn 16:7 KJV)

Thus, for those who would minister "in his name," the time was not right until Pentecost, for the Spirit was not yet given. It was first necessary for Jesus to be "glorified" in his "self-oblation."

> Now this he said about the Spirit, which those who believed in him were to receive; for as yet the Spirit had not been given, because Jesus was not yet glorified.
> (Jn 7:39)

Thus the Pentecostal effusion of the Holy Spirit had already been promised to those who shepherd, by Christ himself, who prayed that the Father would give "another Comforter" who shall "abide" in them.

> And I will pray the Father, and he will give you another Comforter, that he may abide with you forever; even the Spirit of truth.   (Jn 14:17)

It is to this outpouring that St Peter referred as he stood before the multitude which was confounded, amazed and in doubt at the action of the Spirit in those who received him on the day of Pentecost:

> This Jesus God raised up, and of that we all are witnesses. Being therefore exalted at the right hand of God, and his having received from the Father the promise of the Holy Spirit, he has poured out this which you see and hear.   (Acts 2:33)

But in truth, it is only by this outpouring of the Holy

Spirit (promised by Christ and seen in its fulness at Pentecost), that one can speak of any ministry, both of the clergy (shepherds) and the laity.

However, regarding now this activity of the Spirit in relationship to ordination by "the laying on of hands," the best example is found in Timothy:

> Do not neglect the gift (χαρίσματος) you have, which was given you by prophetic utterance when the council of elders laid their hands upon you. Practice these duties, devote yourself to them. (1 Tim 4:14):

And,

> Rekindle the gift of God (τὸ χάρισμα) that is within you through the laying on of my hands; for God did not give us a spirit of timidity (δειλίας) but a spirit of power and love and of self-control.
>
> (2 Tim 1:6-7)

Taken together, the implication in these lines is that Timothy, because he has received ordination "by the laying on of hands," has received thereby these special "gifts" for his ministry of leadership. But it cannot be forgotten that standing within this ordination is teaching and prophecy, by which his leadership function is given in order for him to assume the role of shepherd.

Timothy has been carefully instructed in faith and trained in the *didaskalia* which he exercises; in that training it was clear that he was called to the ministry, that God had imparted to him a gift for its fulfillment; at the same time that gift is looked on as imparted formally through the laying on of hands, authorizing him as an accredited teacher and minister, but used by God as a means of imparting to him a *charisma* for the ministry. The act of laying on of hands has been carried out by Timothy's teacher, Paul, and by the presbytery acting together.[19]

This formal "laying on of hands" means that Timothy has received from Paul and the community a special authorization to proclaim (*kerygma*) and to teach (*didache*) in obedience to the Spirit which Christ promised to pour out upon the leaders of his Church. This is a special charisma, a special gift of the Spirit (which he is to "rekindle"), and which is given with "prayer and the laying on of hands." These two factors are present in the establishment of the diaconal ministry, as well as in Old Testamental ordinations.

It has already been pointed out that in St John's Gospel (Christ's high priestly prayer), this Spirit by which the apostles are ordained draws them within the sphere of Christ's self-consecration. Thus, sharing in his self-consecration, they can minister to others: "As thou didst send me into the world, so I have sent them into the world. And for their sake I consecrate myself, that they also may be consecrated in truth" (Jn 17:18-19).

It is still Christ himself who ordains; ordination is his act. However, Christ, now risen and ascended, has bestowed the Spirit upon his Church, and it is by the "agency" of this Spirit—and in Christ's Body—that the formal laying on of hands is realized. Furthermore, this ordination must be realized in conjunction with Eucharist, as it was by Christ at the Last Supper when he consecrated the twelve to their special ministry as shepherds; his priestly prayer occurs during that supper (cf. Jn 13 ff). This is still the context for ordination today: the celebration of the Eucharist.

Thus it is Christ, the sole celebrant—not the Spirit, not the apostles, not even in this sense, the Church—who bestows this special ministry. It is, however, by the Spirit which he promised, and in the Church which is his Body, that Christ grants the power and efficacy to the one ordained.

This "special" ministry of the clergy, therefore, is not

---

[19]This quote is taken from "The Ministry" in Theological Foundations for Ministry, Ray Andersen, ed. (Grand Rapids, Mich.: Eerdmans Publishing Co. 1979) p. 417.

given by Christ through the Spirit in some sort of "abstraction," or outside the order of his Body. The authorization, which already is considered in the apostolic ministry (e.g. in the case of Timothy) relates this ministry to the obedience and discipline of the Church upon which the Holy Spirit descends at Pentecost. This "shepherding" ministry, even if it is one of leading, is nevertheless always and only one of *service to,* and never one of *ruling over,* any aspect of the Word, the Sacrament or the witness (*martyria*) in the Church. This means that the Word, the Sacrament, and the witness *stand over* the one ordained; they determine him, and not vice-versa. In short, the ministry judges the one who ministers; he is clearly a servant. As Alexander Schmemann says:

> No one can take it upon himself to become a priest, to decide on the basis of his own qualifications, preparation and predispositions. The vocation always comes from above—from God's ordination and order. The priesthood reveals the humility, not the pride of the Church, for it reveals the complete dependence of the Church on Christ's love—that is, on his unique and perfect priesthood. It is not "priesthood" that the priest receives in his ordination, but the gift of Christ's love, that love which made Christ the only Priest and which fills with this unique priesthood, the ministry of those whom He sends to His people.[20]

If this special ministry is one which is "set apart" (and consecration and sanctification mean "set apart"), then it is only by way of the Church which concurs with Christ that ordination should be realized within herself. This is why the exclamation, "worthy" (axios) at the ordination must be one given by the whole Church. The one who ministers, does so not outside nor independent of the Church, but within her as Christ's Body which is animated by the Spirit. In short, it is an act which takes place in the space and time

---

[20]Alexander Schmemann, *Sacraments and Orthodoxy* (Crestwood, NY: St Vladimir's Seminary Press, 1973) p. 94.

which the Holy Spirit creates: the space is that of the Church upon which Christ has placed his name; the time is that of the historical continuity which begins and is carried on by those ordained and consecrated to follow in Christ's own ministry.

Of Laity. It is also in considering this activity of the Holy Spirit, that we come to understand the "general" ministry in the Church, the ministry of the *laity*. If the specific ministry of the clergy is given with the ordination, i.e. the laying on of hands, the ministry of the laity is given at baptism.[21] The activity of the Holy Spirit, however, is central in both ministries, and his activity is clearly to be found in both during the Apostolic era.

"But grace (χάρις) was given to each of us according to the measure of Christ's gift" (Eph 4:7). Thus, *every one* is given this grace which St Paul proceeds to describe, given "for the work of ministry" (ἔργον διακονίας) and "for building up the Body of Christ" (4:12).

This "work of ministry which builds up (edifies) the Body" is a ministry which is of the entire Church; the *charismata* are given to the Body *at large,* and they are to function according to the discernment of that entire Church. It is this which speaks against any arrogance on the part of the clergy; such arrogance only leads to a sclerosis of the Church's life in which the "spirit is quenched" (1 Thess 5:19). If the shepherd is to lead, he is to lead the Body in such a way that these gifts (*charismata*), varied as they are, are brought forth and offered; shepherds are to help these gifts to flourish (not to look upon them out of fear that their use will usurp one's own authority). In short,

[21]It should not be forgotten that in baptism there is also "a laying on of hands" which claims the person for Christ. We have avoided using these terms only for the sake of clarity and distinction between baptism as the general ordination of all Christians, and the specific ordination of the clergy. It can be noted here, however, that there is a difference in those terms used in these two "laying on of hands." The term "heirothesia" (χειρο-θεσία) is the laying on of hands at baptism, when one is ill, or in minor ordinations (literally "the placing of hands"). The other term "heirotonia" (χειροτονία) is the laying on of hands in ordaining persons unto the major orders (deacon, priest, bishop); the latter term is a more dynamic term and has the meaning of stretching forth or extending the hands with definite intention and purpose.

these shepherds, vis-a-vis the ministry of the laity, are to guide (for what else does a shepherd do?) all charismata to their proper service in the Church, and for the world.

These charismata cannot be thought of as any less than, or different from, or even opposite to, this function on the part of the clergy; such thoughts only lead to a clergy vs. laity dichotomy, which is already a veritable "pathology" within the Church.

> And if someday a science which has been long over-due—pastoral pathology—is taught in the seminaries, its first discovery might be that some "clerical voca-tions" are in fact rooted in a morbid desire for that "supernatural respect," especially when the chances of a "natural" one are slim. Our secular world "re-spects" clergy as it "respects" cemeteries: both are needed, both are sacred, both are out of life.[22]

There is no "first team" or "second team," that is, one ministry which is "better" than the other (presumably, this means in the popular sense, that the clergy are the "first team," the laity the "second team"). They belong together, and in a sense, explain each other within the one Body.

This ministry of the laity in which every one is given his gift, is granted in baptism. To understand this, one must begin with this thought: "One has died for all; there-fore all have died" (2 Cor 5:14). Christ died on the Cross, but it is through baptism that we are first made one with him in his death; we all participate in his "self-oblation" in baptism, being drawn into—initiated into—his work of sal-vation. We are grafted into his Body: "as many as have been baptized into Christ have put on Christ" (Gal 3:27 KJV). Being thus baptized into Christ and "putting on Christ," means that one is entered into his "service" (min-istry). To serve in this way means that one does not live for himself, but only for Christ: "And he died for all, that those who live might live no longer for themselves but for him who for their sake, died and was raised" (2 Cor 5:15).

[22]*Ibid.*, Schmemann, p. 92.

Thus the fruit of baptism is obedient service—and since all Christians are baptized, this service is theirs: "he died for *all*."

But how can this ministry be served? If this service is not that of the "shepherd," what is it, and where shall it be realized?

First, it is realized *within* in the Church. By baptism we are made members of his Church; in being incorporated into Christ, we are drawn into his Body. In that Body, each member has his own special function of service and support to fulfill.

> We are to grow up in every way into him who is the head, into Christ, from whom the whole Body, joined and knit together by every joint with which it is supplied, when each part is working properly, makes bodily growth and upbuilds itself in love. (Eph 4:16)

The baptized person, therefore, is not merely an "individual," but a member of Christ's Body: "for we are members of his body, of his flesh and of his bones" (Eph 5:31 KJV). This is why each Christian is a "person," and not merely an "individual." A person has his "personhood" only in community, and a *Christian* person has his Christian personhood in the Christian community. This member, who is now "formed" as a Christian person through baptism, has a direct relationship to Christ who is the head of the Body, and from him the whole Body draws its increase and growth; we "grow up in every way into him who is the head, into Christ" (Eph 4:15).

The ministry of the laity, therefore, is one in which the person, through baptism, is given a "variety of gifts," gifts that differ according to the grace given at baptism:

> Having gifts that differ according to the grace given to us, let us use them.   (Rom 12:6)

In turn, as there are a "variety of gifts," even so there are a "variety of ministries."

> Now there are varieties of gifts (χαρισμάτων), but
> the same spirit; and there are varieties of service
> (διακονιῶν) but the same Lord; and there are
> varieties of working (ἐνεργημάτων), but it is the
> same God who inspires them all in every one.
>
> (1 Cor 12:4-5)

It may therefore be said that, if there are a "variety of
ministries" which baptism gives, and which include both
the clergy and laity within the Church (for one cannot be
ordained to the clergy unless he is first baptized as a Christian layman), then they are held together "by the same
Spirit," and "by the same Lord," that is, it is "the same
God who inspires all in every one." This is precisely how,
in the Church, there is a conjoint ministry, a "symphony,"
to "equip the saints for the work of ministry" (Eph 4:12).

The ministry of the laity can certainly manifest itself in
mission, in teaching, in service within the Body, in philan-
thropic works of the Church, etc. Furthermore, even in teaching mathematics, or working in industry or in politics, a
baptized person can be led toward a saint's life in the
midst of the secular world, can be a Samaritan healing a
wounded man on a highway, can be the mother teaching her
children. But in whatever form this gift of lay ministry is
lived, St Paul reminds us of the condition which makes it, in
fact, a "ministry":

> It is Christ which we proclaim. We admonish everyone
> without distinction, we instruct everyone in all the
> ways of wisdom, so as to present each one of you as
> a mature member of Christ's Body. (Col 2:28 KJV)

As "mature members of his Body," those who minister
as the laity are given to the Church in order "to mend
nets," "to adjust," "to put in order," "to equip for the
fight." This they do as those who were first baptized, i.e.
those who "devoted themselves to the apostles' teaching
and fellowship, to the breaking of bread and the prayers"
(Acts 2:42). They are now "evangelists," as they live their

lives in the Body, in their places of work and in their neigh-
borhoods. As much as are the clergy, they are "ambassadors"
and "representatives" of the Church's total ministry, in which
they act *pars pro toto,* part representing the whole. In this
sense, they "spontaneously" represent Christ.

If the ministry of the shepherd means being "set apart"
within the Body, then the ministry of the laity means being
"set apart" within the world. Thus, being "set apart" from
the world, the laity cannot be caught in the "inertia" of the
working of "this world"; conflict and struggle with the
world, which is fallen, is inevitable. And yet, while living
and ministering in that world, they are to remember and
witness to the fact that they are "chosen," "royal," "holy";
that they indeed are "God's own people." St Peter speaks
to this ministry, saying:

> But you are a chosen race, a royal priesthood, a holy
> nation, God's own people; that you may declare the
> wonderful deeds of him who called you out of dark-
> ness into his marvelous light.   (1 Pet 2:9)

Being now "set apart," they become a "people," an "inheritance," by the mercy of God. In fact, Peter claims that
before this mercy they were *not* a "people."

> Once you were no people but now you are God's
> people (οὐ λαός, νῦν δὲ λαὸς Θεοῦ); once you
> had not received mercy but now you have received
> mercy.   (1 Pet 2:10)

In truth, this ministry of the laity is the first ministry
upon which any subsequent ministry is built. Baptism is, in
a sense, a "once and for all" ordination for all persons (in
the Orthodox liturgy of baptism there is a "laying on of
hands," i.e. an "ordination"). Every priest, then, also belongs to the laity, if by this term we mean *laikos,* the people,
or the *laos tou Theou* (the people of God). By extension, of
course, the priest is also "set apart" from the world.

All this shows us why it is wrong and misleading to define

the laity as being *over against* the clergy. The basic and general ministry given in baptism does not exclude the special ordination into the ranks of the clergy and, in fact, is a prerequisite to it. Consequently, one is first "set apart" from the world ("dead unto sin"), and then is able to be subsequently "set apart" *within* the Body as a special service to that Body.

Thus, it is from this ministry of the laity that the baptized person is also *sent* (ἀπέστειλεν): "Go therefore..." (Mt 28:19). The ministry of the baptized person is served wherever in the world there is room for his "ministry." If he is "set apart" from the world in baptism, it is only to *return* to that world as a servant of Christ who came "for the life of the world." In the secular world the baptized person praises God by the way he lives and works. His ministry is one of manifesting Christ's love:

> I appeal to you therefore, brethren, by the mercies of God, to present your bodies as a living sacrifice, holy and acceptable to God, which is your spiritual worship.
>
> (Rom 12:1)

Both ministries, therefore, are needed to fully describe the one ministry of the Church, the ministry of all believers. "Sacrifice" is the term that best describes this ministry, for the Church is itself a sacrifice (Rom 12:1; 15:16; Phil 2:17), presented to God as holy, good, acceptable and perfect. Persons who offer this sacrifice in both ministries are described by St Paul (1 Cor 3:18-4:13; 2 Cor 4:1-15 and 5:14-6:10) as "servants of Christ," "stewards of the mysteries of God," "like men sentenced to death," "a spectacle to the world," "fools for Christ's sake," "weak," "in disrepute," "hungry and thirsty," "ill-clad, buffeted and homeless," "enduring when persecuted." In this, nothing can be said of the second ministry (clergy) which does not include the first (laity); it is the ministry *of* Christ, *through* the Spirit, *in* the Body, and *for* the salvation of the world.

With this, we return to where we began: with the ministry of the Great Shepherd, Jesus Christ. We are "captives"

in his ministry, in the priesthood of his "self-oblation,"
that is,

> Captives in Christ's triumphal procession, God uses
> us everywhere to reveal and spread abroad the fra-
> grance of the knowledge of himself. We are indeed
> incense offered by Christ to God.
>
> (2 Cor 2:14ff KJV)

CHAPTER THREE

The Person and Role of the Shepherd in the Church

By the fourth century, the triadic ministry of the clergy (bishop, presbyter, deacon), as we know it today, was fully developed. There are, of course, movements toward this full development earlier, i.e. in the second and third centuries. This can be seen in such patristic sources as the Letter of Clement to the Church of Corinth (c. 95 A.D.), the letters of Ignatius of Antioch (c. 107 A.D.), the writings of Justin the Martyr (c. 110-165 A.D.), as well as *The Didache* and *The Shepherd of Hermas* (circa. 100-140), and later (in the third century) the *Apostolic Tradition* of Hippolytus and *The Didascalia* (one can also include, here, Origen and Tertullian).[1] We will deal, however, with the fourth century writings, when the formulation seems fully developed, and under which most of what was earlier written and said can be subsumed. Furthermore, since the effort thus far has been to relate the points of this study to the contemporary ministry, at the point where such connections can be made, it seems most appropriate to move directly to the fourth century, i.e. where such connections with the triadic ministry are most obvious.

The three great hierarchs of the fourth century: St Basil the Great, St Gregory Nazianzen, and St John Chrysostom,

[1] These can be found in any one of the well-known sources, e.g. *Ancient Christian Writers* (ed. Quasten et al.) and/or *Patrologia Graeca* and *Patrologia Latina* by Migne, and/or the *Ante-Nicean Fathers* (Eerdmans).

were among the fathers who devoted much of their writings
to the question of ministry and shepherding. In order to set
the context for their thoughts, a brief commentary will introduce each of these Fathers, but the reader should remember that the concern here is not an historical, nor doctrinal
one (which would entail a different and more detailed approach than our study) but only what they believed and
said about the ministry of the Church.

1. The Person of the Shepherd— St Gregory Nazianzen

The first of the Three Hierarchs who speaks of the
ministry of the shepherd is St Gregory Nazianzen, called the
"Theologian." After being "forcibly" ordained by his father,
who was a bishop (Gregory the Elder), Gregory fled to
the side of St Basil (c. 361) for refuge, believing that since
he did not want to be a priest, an injustice was inflicted upon
him. For the present study, most of what he says about the
priesthood is taken from his famous *Oration on the Flight
to Pontus,* which he presented to the people of Nazianzus
when he returned from that flight, now as a priest. This
oration appears as a type of apology and explanation as to
why he fled, and what it is about the awesomeness of the
priesthood that caused his flight. Gregory is concerned with
the level of "priestly consciousness" (*hieratiki syneithesis*),
the awareness or discernment of what it means to be a
priest. For example, although any person would want to
flee from the heavy burden, but stays because of the Church's
mission, each candidate must still ask himself: "Am I
worthy?"[2] (*Apol. Orat.* 10, P.G. 35:420). This is the true

---

[2]In truth, I am indebted to these two sources which serve to inspire
and capsulize these thoughts on these three hierarchs: "The Image of the
Priest According to the Three Hierarchs" by Lewis Patsavos which he uses
in the *Greek Orthodox Theological Review,* Vol. XXI, Spring, 1976, pp.
55-70 from which this quote is taken (which is also true of the section on
Basil the Great and John Chrysostom), and the excellent book *solely* based
on leadership in St Basil: *The Church and the Charisma of Leadership in
Basil of Caesarea* by Paul J. Fedwick (Pontifical Institute of Mediaeval
Studies, Toronto, 1979), Chapters 2 and 3. (*The Ascetic Works,* abbreviated

"identity" question of the priesthood and Gregory seeks to explain it by considering four aspects: the shepherd as *doctor* in pastoral care, the *maturity* and *propriety* of the shepherd, the proper *teaching* of *doctrine* and the need for a proper *training* and *experience*. Each of these is relevant to us in the contemporary ministry.

Shepherd as Doctor in Pastoral Care

Gregory very directly addresses the term "shepherd" when he presents the defense of his flight to Pontus. For him, the consciousness of the priesthood is a consciousness of Christ, who is "a Shepherd to shepherds," and a "Guide to guides." Here St Gregory's prayer is that he, being guided by Christ, will in turn be able to guide the flock in order that Christ will "present to himself, his flock" worthy of heaven. In this way, Gregory sees how the priest, as disciple, is to be transparent to Christ, as master.

> Such is my defence: its reasonableness I have set forth: and may the God of peace himself hold me by my right hand, and guide me with his counsel, and receive me with glory, who is a Shepherd to shepherds and a Guide to guides: that we may feed his flock with knowledge, and not with the instruments of a foolish shepherd; according to the blessing, and not according to the curse pronounced against the men of former days. May he give strength and power unto his people, and himself present to himself his flock resplendent and spotless and worthy of the fold on high . . . so that in his temple everyone, both flock and shepherds together may say, "Glory, in Christ Jesus our Lord, to whom be all glory for ever and ever. Amen." (NPNF, p. 228)[3]

by Fedwick as *Reg. fus. Reg. br.* and *Reg. mor.*, [*Moral Rules*] are the Clarke translations, while the *Homilies* are Migne's translation). These are the ones that I use in this section on St Basil, and are included immediately in the text.

[3]P. Schaff and H. A. Wace, *A Select Library of Nicene and Post-Nicene*

In establishing this connection between the shepherd and the Great Shepherd, Gregory uses the lofty language of the theology of "the image of God." He accomplishes this in describing the shepherd as a doctor who heals, but whose healing is accomplished when he leads the flock back to God. In short, the shepherd's "art" is to lead to "deification" (*Theosis*). By confronting the condition of the image of God in man, the person is guided to be a "god through communion with God." This is what Gregory means by "healing."

> But the aim of the (priestly, as opposed to medical) art is to provide the soul with wings to rescue it from the world, and to present it to God. It consists in preserving the image of God in man, if it exists; in strengthening it, if it is in danger; in restoring it, if it has been lost. Its end is to make Christ dwell in the heart through the Spirit, and, in short, to make a god sharing heavenly bliss out of him who belongs to the heavenly host.   (NPNF, p. 209)

But when he directly refers to "healing," Gregory speaks of the need for the shepherd's *own* healing, as well as the healing of others. It is here where Gregory deals at the level of priestly consciousness and identity.

> Of this healing we, who are set over others, are the ministers and fellow-labourers; for whom it is a great thing to recognize and heal, first of all, our own passions and sicknesses: ... but a much greater thing is the power to heal and skillfully cleanse those of others, to the advantage both of those who are in need of healing and of those whose charge it is to heal.
>   (NPNF, p. 210)

Fathers of the One Christian Church. Series 2, vol. VII, S. Cyril of Jerusalem, S. Gregory Nazianzen: Orations, Sermons, etc. (Grand Rapids: W. B. Eerdman's Publishing Company, 1955) pp. 203-227. Hereafter this source will be referred to simply as *NPNF* in the text on Nazianzus. The quotes which are used are taken directly from his second oration *On the Flight* (pp. 203-227), out of his forty-five, many of which are purely aimed at a theological defense against heresy.

This capacity to be such a healer, however, depends not only on the shepherd's avoidance of things, but on the effort to strive positively towards something.

> But in the case of man, hard as it is for him to learn how to submit to rule, it seems far harder to know how to rule over men, and hardest of all is this ruling power of ours; its risk is ... proportionate to its height and dignity. . . . Although a man has kept himself pure from sin. . . . I do not know that this is sufficient for one who is to instruct others in virtue. For he who has received this charge, not only needs to be free from evil ... but also to be eminent in good. . . . He should know no limits in goodness or spiritual progress, and should dwell upon the loss of what is still beyond him, rather than the gain of what he has attained ... and not think it a great gain to excel ordinary people, but a loss to fall short of what we ought to be.   (NPNF, p. 207)

In the contemporary ministry of the shepherd, the same possibility of risk exists when the pastor easily forgets that even the "authority" of his leadership is, always and only, to be one of "service" (ministry), *and not of power!* Our Lord made this very clear in his teaching of the disciples (e.g. Mk 10:42-45). In this service, Gregory says the shepherd is to be superior to the ordinary person *in virtue,* but he is never to consider himself better because of this. Furthermore, the shepherd must struggle constantly toward the "ought"; anything less is a loss to himself.

Because he has this elevated but still humble position, the shepherd, as Gregory says, must also keep *balance.* He cannot afford to be enslaved to the many passions with which he is tempted because of his powerful position. The sad possibility is that he will be dragged by such a passion either to one side or the other, and then, he will fall from that elevated position. This "balance" is required for any definition of proper pastoral care today, and as St Gregory describes it, is even like "walking a tight rope." The pastor must know this to properly care for his flock:

> This, however, I take to be generally admitted—that just as it is not safe for those who walk on a lofty tight rope to lean to either side, their safety depends upon their perfect balance: so in the case of one of us, if he leans to either side (whether from vice or ignorance), no slight danger of a fall into sin is incurred, both for himself and those who are led by him. But we must really walk in the King's highway, and take care not to turn aside from it either to the right hand or to the left, as the Proverbs say. For such is the case with our passions, and such in this matter is the task of the good shepherd, if he is to know properly the souls of his flock, and to guide them according to the methods of a pastoral care which is right and just, and worthy of our true Shepherd.
>
> (NPNF, p. 211, 212, 224, 227)

It is only if the shepherd remembers his proper position and identity—and keeps this balance—that the full definition of the "one body" can be preserved. St Gregory, again in defining a proper pastoral care, sets it in this context of both clergy and the laity—both with their own "ministries" and according to the variety of the Spirit's gifts. If they "combine and knit together by the harmony of the Spirit," they can realize a true unity and form one body. Order (τάξις) is, of course, required, in which one must guide, and the other be guided.

> Now, just as in the body there is one member which guides and presides, while another is guided over and subject; so too in the churches, God has ordained ... (and) has knit all together, that those for whom such treatment is beneficial, should be subject to pastoral care and rule (i.e. be guided by word and deed in the path of duty), while others should be pastors and teachers, for the perfecting of the church. This

> God has done in order that both may be so united
> and compacted together, that, although one is lacking
> and another is pre-eminent, they may, like the mem-
> bers of our bodies, be so combined and knit together
> by the harmony of the Spirit, as to form one perfect
> body, really worthy of Christ himself, our Head.
>
> (NPNF, p. 205)

But St Gregory still feels the need to explain—even
apologetically—just why it is necessary for some persons to
be the leaders, or as he says, why they are called to a
"ministry of leadership" (from which he fled). Furthermore,
not everyone should *want* to be the shepherd. The Church
simply cannot realize her mission if nobody accepted to be
such a leader, and if nobody accepted to be led. Gregory
makes his final point for order in the Body by referring to
the liturgical rites.

> I am aware then that anarchy and disorder cannot be
> more advantageous than order and rule, either to
> other creatures or to men; . . . Since this seems right
> and just, it is, I take it, equally wrong and disorderly
> that all should wish to rule, and that no one should
> accept it. For if all men were to shirk this office,
> whether it must be called a ministry or a leadership,
> the fair fulness of the Church would be halting in
> the highest degree, and in fact cease to be fair. And
> further, where, and by whom would God be wor-
> shipped among us in those mystic and elevating rites
> which are our greatest and most precious privilege, if
> there were neither king, nor governor, nor priesthood,
> nor sacrifice, nor all those highest offices to the loss
> of which, for their great sins, men of old were con-
> demned in consequence of their disobedience?
>
> (NPNF, p. 205)

Maturity and Propriety of the Shepherd

The shepherd, who is to cure like a doctor, needs a sense of maturity and propriety in terms of "place, time, age and season"; he must apply the medicine to the flock according to what they are able to sustain. There are various characteristics and requirements of such maturity and propriety, and these again are seen in the context of the priestly consciousness and identity. Gregory knows that what the flock (or to use his medical language, "the sick") wants and desires, cannot be granted if it interferes ("is a hindrance") with the art of healing.

> Place and time and age and season and the like, are the subjects of a physician's scrutiny; he will prescribe medicines and diet, and guard against things injurious, that the desires of the sick may not be a hindrance to his art. Sometimes, and in certain cases, he will make use of the cautery or the knife or even the severer remedies; but none of these, laborious and hard as they may seem, is so difficult as the diagnosis and cure of our habits, passions, lives, wills and whatever else is within us ... and establishing in their stead what is gentle and dear to God, ... not allowing the superior to be overpowered by the inferior, which would be the greatest injustice ...
>
> (NPNF, p. 208)

But to be able to know how and when to apply this spiritual medicine to the wrong and evil "habits, passions, lives, wills and whatever else is within us," simply cannot be realized in the inexperience and haste of youth. Again, a sense of propriety and maturity is needed, and age and experience are part of this requirement. This obviously is the rationale for those canons of the Church which speak of "age" as a requirement for ordination (at least by implication).

For white hairs combined with prudence are better

than inexperienced youth; well-reasoned hesitation is better than inconsiderate haste; and a brief reign is better than a long tyranny. Just as a small portion honourably won, is better than considerable possessions which are dishonourable and uncertain, so a little gold is better than a great weight of lead, and a little light is better than much darkness.

(NPNF, p. 219)

Obviously, as Gregory now concentrates on the identity of the priesthood in terms of his awareness, maturity, propriety, etc., he does not circumvent some of those elements of which this identity is formed; such an identity is shaped in pain, which is the only way to grow (not intellectually, but precisely in terms of "consciousness"). He knows that an "internal warfare" must be fought within the shepherd. Indeed, this is painful, since it is one which deals with "the passions" and the "purifying of the mind." This qualification is also needed by today's shepherds who must likewise "contend"; Gregory sees this as a prerequisite for one "who is entrusted with the rule of souls or the office of mediator" between God and man.

I have said nothing yet of the internal warfare within ourselves, and in our passions, in which we are engaged night and day ... either secretly or openly, and against the tide which tosses and whirls us hither and thither, and by the aid of our senses and other sources of pleasures of this life; so that it is difficult for anyone ... to overcome the depressing power of matter. And before a man has, as far as possible, gained this superiority, and sufficiently purified his mind, I do not think it safe for him to be entrusted with the rule over souls or the office of mediator (for such, I take it, a priest is between God and man).

(NPNF, p. 222)

This propriety and maturity, which is developed precisely in "internal warfare," is nothing which the person can acquire alone; it is clearly one's response to the Holy Spirit, with which the person cooperates.

> For I know that I am too weak for this warfare, and therefore turned my back, hiding my face in the rout, and sat solitary, because I was filled with bitterness and sought to be silent, understanding that it is an evil time.   (NPNF, p. 222)

Consequently, if ministry is not realized in cooperation with the Holy Spirit, if it is done only by one's own will or is negligent of God's grace, then *despair* in the ministry is bound to be the result. "Pelegianism" (self-will) not only leads to pride, but also to *despair,* since one's own efforts, apart from grace, will always fail in the life of the pastor. Here the spiritual lesson of each Christian takes on a special impact for the shepherd: nothing we accomplish on our own can ever totally satisfy our hearts; though we may search for "idols" (whatever they may be) to find such satisfaction, our hearts are made for Christ. This is no different for the shepherd who reaches maturity in the awareness (consciousness) of what are both his great possibilities and his limits. His own effort *is* crucial, but he is not to suffer from grandiose ideas from which he is bound to be "let down" and "burned out." What better definition is there of "maturity"? Gregory remembers when he has failed in properly responding to his position as shepherd:

> With these thoughts I am occupied night and day: they waste my marrow and feed upon my flesh and will not allow me to be confident or to look up. They depress my soul, and abase my mind, and fetter my tongue, and make me consider, not the position of a prelate, or the guidance and direction of others, . . . but how I myself am to escape the wrath to come, and to scrape off from myself somewhat of the rust of vice.   (NPNF, p. 219)

But when the shepherd does indeed respond, when his

will and God's grace converge (cooperate), maturity is the result, and it is that maturity, painful as it is to reach, that the shepherd needs in order to direct the flock. The Theologian cuts directly to the identity of the priest as shepherd with these words:

> A man must himself be cleansed, before cleansing others: himself become wise, that he may make others wise; become light, and then give light: draw near to God, and so bring others near; be hallowed, then hallow them; be possessed of hands, to lead others by the hand; be of wisdom to give wisdom (advice).
>
> (NPNF, p. 219)

The Shepherd and Teaching of Doctrine

The aforementioned maturity and propriety, Gregory says, is also needed in the proper distribution of the word and in the teaching of doctrine. Great "spiritual power" is needed in order to "give in due season," and to "regulate with judgment the truth of our opinions." This is required because of the tremendous scope of the shepherd's concern, since he must deal with "such subjects" as are most weighty.

> In regard to the distribution of the word (to mention last the first of our duties), i.e., of that divine and exalted word, which everyone now is ready to discourse upon; if anyone else bodily undertakes it and supposes it within the power of every man's intellect, I am amazed at his intelligence, not to say his folly. To me indeed it seems no slight task, and one requiring no little spiritual power, to give in due season, to take from his portion of the word, and to regulate with judgment the truth of our opinions, which are concerned with such subjects as the world or worlds, matter, soul, mind, intelligent natures, better or worse, providence which . ... seeks in our experience of it, to

be governed according to some principle, but one which
is at variance with those of earth and of men.
                                        (NPNF, p. 212)

Gregory then speaks directly about the problem of when
to teach these doctrines, and the very importance of the
proper doctrine in the life of the flock.

Accordingly, to impress the truth upon a soul when
it is still fresh, like wax not yet subjected to the
seal, is an easier task than inscribing pious doctrine
on the top of inscriptions—I mean wrong doctrine and
dogmas—with the result that the former are confused and thrown into disorder by the latter.... a
soul to be written upon should be free from the in-
scription of harmful doctrines . . . Otherwise the pious
inscriber would have a twofold task: the erasure of
the former impressions and the substitution of others
which are more excellent, and more worthy to abide.
                                        (NPNF, pp. 213-214)

It seems clear to St Gregory that one must teach properly
from the start. This is clearly the responsibility of the shepherd, one who is to pastor the flock so that they do not
"mix" proper doctrine with what is "cheap, debased, stale
and tasteless." This the shepherd might be tempted to
do "for his own profit (or) to accommodate himself (or)
to acquire favor (or) to serve their own pleasures," all in
order "to gain the special good will of the multitude." For
this, of course, he will be held responsible, since this is like
"shedding the innocent blood of simpler souls."
                                        (NPNF, p. 214)

The Need for Training and Experience

For the proper teaching, however, one must first be
taught himself. If the shepherd undertakes such an effort
without this proper training, St Gregory says, this is either
folly or rashness:

Accordingly, to undertake the training of others before being sufficiently trained oneself, and to learn as men, say, the potter's art on a wine-jar, that is, to practice ourselves in piety at the expense of others' souls, seems to me to be excessive folly or excessive rashness—folly, if we are not even aware of our own ignorance; rashness if in spite of this knowledge we venture on the task. (NPNF, p. 216)

Until the time that one is properly trained, in fact, it is better for that novice to go to those who "are more skillful," i.e. others who know the doctrine and are experienced. These, Gregory claims, are our "advisors" and teachers, to whom we should listen: "to give a kindly hearing":

After a discussion of these points with advisors who ... wish us well, we will prefer to learn those canons of speech and action which we did not know, rather than undertake to teach them in our ignorance. For it is delightful to have the reasoning of the aged come to one even until the depth of old age, able, as it is, to aid a soul new to piety. (NPNF, p. 216)

Indeed, "it is delightful to have the reasoning," but Gregory also knows that, in the end, "treatment" is not simply a case of knowing, cognitively, what are the doctrines (important as they are), or even, knowing what are the "virtues and vices"; treatment, rather, requires the "actual experience and practice" of the shepherd (NPNF, p. 211). Obviously this can serve as a model for the training of pastors (shepherds) in our contemporary ministry.

Such training which includes both the "exact views" of doctrine, and the "actual experience," is a challenge to contemporary pastoral training in terms of a total, "wholistic" education. This type of education is indeed one of a priestly consciousness which, Gregory says, requires a "depth of the earth" and cannot be acquired "speedily" (so that the seeds "blow away," or are in any sense, fragile).

What is needed in order to form, not a child, but a mature servant who will be the "King of the city," is a solid "foundation." After all, Gregory says, this shepherd will

> take a stand with angels, and give glory with arch-angels, and cause the sacrifice to ascend to the altar on high, and share the priesthood of Christ, and re-new the creature, and set forth the image, and create inhabitants for the world above, aye and, greatest of all, *be* God, and make *others* to be God.
>
> (NPNF, p. 220)

Can such a position demand anything less than that train-ing which forms a total "priestly consciousness"? This priest, in order to make others, by grace and communion, "one with God," cannot be prepared hastily and by short cuts.

The growth of the shepherd never stops; even after his initial training he is to grow steadily and continuously, like "the common sailor grows to be the helmsman," or like "the brave soldier grows to be the general":

> Nor indeed is it strange or inconsistent for the majority of those who are devoted to the study of divine things, to ascend to rule from being ruled, nor does it over-step the limits laid down by philosophy, or involve disgrace; any more than for an excellent sailor to become a lookout-man, and for a lookout-man, who has successfully kept watch over the winds, to be entrusted with the helm; or, if you will, for a brave soldier to be made a captain, and a good captain to become a general.   (NPNF, p. 206)

St Gregory, then, knowing that both the initial and complete training is required, and that further, this training continues in the life of the shepherd, claims that this is needed so that he can become—and continue to be—a good "model" for the flock. He warns in two places what will be the result if the shepherd is a poor model: first he will "undertake to heal others while he himself is still full of sores," and secondly, this poor model will be guilty of those same things which our Lord found wrong about Pharisees.

> This then is the first point in what we have said, which it is right for us to guard against: being ... poor models for the people, or barely escaping the proverb that we undertake to heal others while ourselves are full of sores. (NPNF, p. 207)

To this he adds:

> I am alarmed by the reproaches of the Pharisees, the conviction of the scribes. For it is disgraceful for us who ought to greatly surpass them ... (i.e. Pharisees and scribes) if we desire the kingdom of heaven, to be found more deeply sunk in vice. When this happens we deserve to be called "serpents, a generation of vipers, and blind guides, who strain out a gnat and swallow a camel," or sepulchres foul within, in spite of our external comeliness, or platters outwardly clean, and everything else which they are, or which is laid to their charge. (NPNF, p. 219)

Gregory seems appalled at those shepherds who "intrude into the most sacred offices," and who are truly unworthy and rash in their assumptions about what it means to be ordained. He is ashamed of such behavior and does not himself want to practice it. Such persons want the "position of authority," not as a means for virtue, but as "a means of livelihood." They, obviously, have not realized that this is "a ministry of which they must give account":

> I was influenced besides by another feeling, whether base or noble I do not know, but I will speak out to you all my secrets. I was ashamed of all those others, who, without being better than ordinary people ... intrude into the most sacred offices; and, before becoming worthy to approach the temples, they lay claim to the sanctuary, and they push and thrust

around the holy table, as if they thought this order
to be a means of livelihood instead of a pattern of
virtue, or an absolute authority instead of a ministry
of which we must give account. In fact they are almost
more in number than those whom they govern; ... and
unfortunate in their dignity; so that, it seems to me,
as time and this evil alike progress, they will not have
any one left to rule!   (NPNF, pp. 206-207)

And what must the shepherd be in order to present a
proper example or "model"? Only the one who knows
that he is, first of all, *not worthy* of this ministry, or even
of "the name of priest." It is for this reason that Gregory
fled after his ordination; he knew himself unworthy of
this sacrifice:

Since then I knew these things, and that no one is
worthy of the mightiness of God, nor the sacrifice, nor
the priesthood, who has not first presented himself
to God, a living, holy sacrifice, and set forth the
reasonable, well-pleasing service, and sacrificed to God
the sacrifice of praise and the contrite spirit which
is the only sacrifice required of us by the Giver of
all, how could I dare to offer to Him the external
sacrifice, the antitype of the great mysteries, or clothe
myself with the garb and name of priest, before my
hands had been consecrated by holy works.

(NPNF, p. 223)

Thus, for St Gregory of Nazianzus, this "priestly consciousness," which he emphasizes continuously as the crucial
ingredient in the identity of the pastor, is founded upon
nothing less than such a "sacrifice." In short, this "consciousness" unfolds in the fruit of sacrifice and, thus, in true
ministry.

Finally, however, there is nothing that will truly "qual-
ify" the shepherd. He can never accept this appointment
"eagerly," but only with trepidation and fear. Of all people,

St Gregory the Theologian knows it is only by the grace of God that one becomes the shepherd:

> Who is the man who, although he has never applied himself to, nor learnt to speak the hidden wisdom of God in a mystery, although he is still a babe, still fed with milk, still of those who are not numbered in Israel, ... although he is not yet able to take up the Cross of Christ like a man, although he is possibly not yet one of the more honorable members, yet will joyfully and eagerly accept his appointment as head of the fulness of Christ? No one, if he will listen to my judgment and accept my advice! This is extremist of dangers in the eyes of everyone who understands the magnitude of success, or the utter ruin of failure.   (NPNF, p. 224)

2. St Basil on the Shepherd

St Basil the Great is remembered for being an organizer of the monastic life and for his insistence on a true philanthropy. He is also concerned for the qualifications and virtues of the Christian life in general, but has much to say about those specific to the shepherd. The shepherd, as leader of the Church, must serve as a model of these qualifications and virtues. Lewis Patsavos explains why this is true:

> From the first half of the fourth century it was becoming customary to select bishops from among the monks distinguished for their holiness and learning. Many of the qualifications defined for monks apply equally to candidates for the priesthood, particularly for promotion to the rank of bishop. A careful study of these ascetic writings reveals that the fundamental virtues which should grace the shepherd of souls should be: love of God, love of flock, humility, meekness and tolerance.[4]

[4]*Ibid.*, Patsavos, p. 59.

Patsavos then explains in detail what each of these virtues means to St Basil in light of our present concern for the ministry of the shepherd. In order to understand how St Basil views the role of the shepherd, one must focus upon the one word which he himself uses to describe that role: προεστὼς (*Proestos* = leader). He does not take this word *proestos* lightly. He uses this term to describe the leader seven times in his small *Asceticon* (*Ascetic Works*) and about fifty times in his great *Asceticon*.

When Basil writes these *Ascetic Works*—which elaborate on his concept of the monastic community (which was the communal or *cenobitic* style, rather than the *eremitic* style), he offers a very valuable contribution, a prototype, as to how we are to live in the Church "in the world." His use of the word *askesis* refers not only to the "ascetical struggle" of the solitary figure in the desert, but to the struggle of the Christian life in general. With this view only, these following points are developed.

What is this "leader" here for? He is to make of the followers what he calls "complete Christians" (οἱ τέλειοι Χριστιανοί).[5] Such "complete Christians" are to be developed in both the ascetic community and the local church. Furthermore each local body of the Church is "complete"; it is but the manifestation of a universal reality (*On Psalm 48,1*). The shepherd is to lead each local community with this concept in mind.

In his *On Psalm 28* he speaks about the scope of responsibility of this shepherd (leader):

> ... such are the leaders of the disciples of Christ. They lead them forth to ... nourishment of doctrine, (they) water them with living water ... (they) raise them up and they nurture them until they produce fruit: then they guide them to rest and safety. ...
>
> (*On Psalm 28:2*)

[5]This term is used by John Meyendorff in "St Basil, Messalianism and Byzantine Christianity" in *St Vladimir's Theological Quarterly* (vol. 24, no. 4, 1980) pp. 219-234.

Note here that the leaders are not only disciples them-selves, but they are the leaders of other disciples; each of the people (the *laos*) are the "disciples of Christ" and this leader is to "nourish" them, "water" them, "raise them up," and "guide" them. In fact, it is this leader who is there precisely to lead these Christians to their "completion," which is to make of each of them a disciple. For the shepherd today, this is the same: an awesome and fearful responsibility, and it remains for us the focus of our contemporary challenge.

In light of this view, the question of the contemporary shepherd becomes: "How does St Basil see us doing that?" Or it can be asked, by extension: "How does the contemporary priest as shepherd see himself being able to do that, i.e. make complete Christians, make disciples of Christ?" To answer this question we must investigate two particular aspects: the context of the Church, and the particular characteristics of the leader in that context.

The Context of the Church

The leadership function needs the context which dis-tinguishes it, at once, as a Christian and pastoral function, and that context, of course, is the Church. The Church is the "calling out" and the "gathering" of Christians; the Greek word *Ekklesia* (*ek*-out, *klesis*-calling) means exactly this.

The shepherd must know that he does not have the luxury of choosing whom he will or will not lead of those who are "called out." St Basil says that nobody is to be left out and he is very specific in showing this. In *On Psalm 48:1,* he speaks of this inclusivity by referring to "three pairs" of people. He says:

There are three pairs of those called in which every race of man is included. Among these are
1. non-Romans and Roman citizens (which refers to the broadest scope of social status)
2. primitive people and civilized people
3. the rich and the poor

And why? So that we would not fail, he says, to offer to each person, the church's aid in the path to salvation.

Within this context St Basil tells us that the leadership of the Church is built upon a "simplicity" (ἁπλότης); here he uses the term which also means a "singleness," a "frankness." He is not implying in this term "simplicity" that the leader has a "simple" job or task, or that it can be reduced to one thing or another. Rather, the implication is that all the multiple forms, efforts, functions, etc. of the shepherd or leader are rooted in and come out of a "simplicity." What is this simplicity? It is comprised of two parts, each one being crucial:

1. The centrality of Christ and
2. The lack of arrogance and self-sufficiency on the part of the shepherd (*Contra Eunomius* 1:3).

(Eunomius maintained that human beings can know the essence of God; thus, in his arrogance, he lost both of these characteristics.)

The leader of the gathering reveals this "simplicity" in many tasks. There is a multiplicity within the simplicity. In his *Homily 11,* for example, Basil says that neither natural endowments, nor riches, nor strength, nor power, are ends in themselves, but they are instruments, "organs" of virtue. He says that we are not only to use such "organs," but we are also to use "practical wisdom" (φρόνησις), i.e. our human minds, in *applying* them. In *Homily Three,* in fact, St Basil says we must exercise various crafts—"techniques" (τέχναι). These instruments, these crafts which we are to use, are intended for the *good of others* and not for the one who possesses them; they are given to us as outstanding achievements by God in the form of what he calls the "human logos."

This is why in *Homily 11* Basil warns the shepherd not to be envious of these various instruments and crafts of other leaders. He says:

It is your good, and it is for your sake that your

brother was endowed with the gift of teaching, if
only you are willing to accept it . . . why, then, do
you refuse to lend your ears . . . why do you not with
gratitude take advantage of the benefits. (*Hom 11:15*)

The leader, then, must use all these qualities which God
has given him, because of the variety of people he is to
lead. Basil sees the Church, in this sense, as a "house." In
his *Homily 3:4* he very practically says:

In the great house, which is the Church, there are not
only vessels of every kind—gold and silver, wood and
earthenware—there are also manifold lives and talents.
Indeed (the house) houses hunters, travellers, archi-
tects, builders, shepherds, athletes, soldiers.

Each of these must be met, seen, and dealt with as they
are. The "renewal of the mind," he reminds us again in
Homily 29, takes place in each individual, in his own walk
of life, again "in order that no one may be left without (the
Church's) aid."

The scope of the shepherd's concern is even broader
when St Basil refers to the Church, not only as the house,
but as a "city." What must be imagined here, is all the
types, the problems and the individuals in a "city," and
further, the range of care that the shepherd must have in
such a circumstance. The reminder is that one today cannot
reduce the function of the shepherd to any *one* particular
role. In contemporary terms, this tells us that the shepherd
of the community, the leader of the flock, is neither "running
an administration," nor is he a "liturgical robot"; in fact,
St Basil seems to understand liturgy (leitourgia) not only
as worship (προσκύνησις) but sees worship itself as
the heart of the complete *service of the people of God—*
service which includes all our works of love.

There is also in this city a "system" (σύστημα), an
established community built according to the law and fortified by faith (*Homilies 45 and 59*). There is order (τάξις),
there is discipline. Basil sees this as a normal part of a

proper care (ἐπιμέλεια), part of the leadership role or caring role of the pastor in the Church. Within this system, order is needed by the shepherd in order to discern (διακρίνειν) and judge between right and wrong, proper and improper. By this term, it cannot be understood that one discerns according to his own judgment; he is to discern according to the Church's *exousia,* the Church's power and authority. The Church completes such discernment through these "instruments" of the shepherd.

Also within the context of the Church, St Basil speaks of disposition (διάθεσις). Like many other of the Eastern Fathers, St Basil does not believe that we can lead "by force." True leadership cannot be forced on others. If, however, the Church through her leaders cannot "force," what then can be done? How do we as leaders today practice leadership in the context of the Church?

To understand this development, one must go directly to St Basil's concept of *logos spermatikos,* that is, the concept that there are implanted in man from his very beginning, "seeds" (σπέρμα), germs of God, germs of the Logos. In this context, this means that even God himself does not force himself "from the outside," as it were, but rather provides reminders and stimuli to activate and cultivate these inner *logoi,* with which all humans are naturally created (*Ascetics Works 2:1*). If this constituent part of man's nature can be cultivated, it will issue forth only as a "good moral action" (κατόρθωμα) which is love.

It is this which is "natural" to humans (evil being unnatural). Consequently, natural circumstances and relationships in human lives, if accompanied by faith, are then transformed into true acts for the sake of Christ. This is why one cannot be a Christian without being humane (although it is true that one can be a "humanist" without being a Christian—a great danger for the contemporary shepherd). St Basil exhorts the shepherd to remind his flock about this.

For Basil, Christian perfection cannot be individual, but can flourish only in the life of communion with God and one's neighbor. In proposing this corporate cultivation of these inborn seeds of the logos, he says that one is here simply to "wash feet." (A saying popularly attributed to St Basil is: "If I live alone, whose feet will I wash?"). It is clear to him that "God transfers this love from neighbor to himself: 'If you've done it to them, you've done it to me' " (*Ascetic Works* 3:1).

But the point for the shepherd is this: if we cannot *force* this to happen, what then can we do? How can the leader cultivate and activate this tendency toward spiritual development and communion? St Basil says it is for us to create the "disposition," what he calls the διάθεσις, the atmosphere, the environment, the ethos (here he uses the term to ἴδιον) in which this cultivation can indeed happen. With this in mind, he asks in his *Moral Rule 80*, quite logically,

> What is this ethos of a Christian? Faith working through love . . . Not to seek one's own good but the good of the loved one for the benefit of his body and soul.   (*Moral Rule 80:22*)

This environment is reached by a form of separation from the world, but not necessarily the monastic separation from the world (κόσμου ἀναχώρησις). It is a kind of "severance" (μία φυγή) within the soul, i.e. a severance of our soul's sympathy from the wrong things of this life, so "that the heart may readily receive every impression of divine doctrine" (*Letter 2:2*). This is how St Basil bridges the gap in this scheme of asceticism between the monastic life and parish life, both in the quest for the Kingdom. He shifts the separation from the physical and spatial setting to that of the inner disposition of the Christian. The shepherd is the one who leads the flock to this kind of "separation" and "severance" from the world.

St Basil adds the following about this "disposition":

1. No man is individually self-sufficient (αὐτάρκης). By nature he needs others.
                                   (*Ascetic Works* 7:1)

2. The Logos of Christian life does not allow each

man to look to his own good exclusively. "For love," he says "seeketh not his own."

3. It is harmful to the soul when men have no one to rebuke them for their faults.

4. A charisma is a gift of the Holy Spirit given for the benefit of others. No person can possess all the charismata. But "when a number live together, a man enjoys not only his own charisma, but he multiplies it by imparting it to others, and reaps the fruit of *other* men's charismata as if it were his own."

(Ascetic Works 7:2)

5. That in a structure which allows for no personal relations, it is simply impossible to practice Christian virtues, such as humility and mercy. He says Scripture provides the theory for this perfection, but theory without practice is void.

(Ascetic Works 4)

In creating such a "disposition" for "faith to work through love," St Basil tells the shepherd that he can make Christians *disciples and members,* so that they can be *salt and light* for the world. This is how Basil sees the "complete Christians" being formed.

Particular Characteristics of the Leader

What does St Basil lead us to consider about the shepherd himself? What further characteristics must the leader have in order to lead, to preside, to protect, to care?

First Basil tells us that it is not even the Church that gives him the right of ministry; it is God who gives—the Church simply provides the way and the medium for the person to exercise it.

There are various kinds of leadership capacities, and each member in the Church has, to one degree or another, a leading charism which can be offered. However, these charismata are to be seen in an *order* and there are two

parts of this order. One is of oversight—foreseeing and ar-
ranging (like the power of the eye to see)—the other is like
the power of the ear or the hand in hearing what to do, and
doing what must be done (*Reg. fus.* 24). But the pastor
and parishioners—who are entrusted with these leadership
capacities today—need each other to constitute the fullness
of the Body, i.e. the ministry of the clergy and the laity.
Because of this interdependence, however, no leader should
become arrogant and self-sufficient. In his *Epistle 97*, Basil
uses his own bodily constitution to make this point:

> When I look to these my limbs and see that no one
> of them is self-sufficient, how can I reckon myself
> competent to discharge the duties of life? One foot
> cannot walk securely without the other, one eye
> cannot see well without the other; hearing is most
> exact through both ears ... In a word, of all that is
> done by nature and will, I see nothing done without
> the concord of fellow forces. (*Epistle 97*)

So the first warning is that no shepherd should think
that, as the leader of the community at large, he is self-
sufficient.

Basil relates this also to the relationships between shepherds—important for us today between fellow pastors:

> For it is an evil time, a time when some trip up
> their neighbor's heels, some stamp on a man when
> he is down, and others clap their hands with joy,
> that there is none to feel for the fallen, to hold out
> a helping hand (when we should not even pass a
> beast who is fallen). Why not? Because the love of
> many has grown cold; brotherly admonitions are heard
> no more, nowhere is there Christian pity, nowhere
> falls the tear of sympathy.
> (*On the Holy Spirit,* 78)

While he is leading, says Basil, the shepherd should
know that not everything is written in scripture for us, not

every little factor is covered for us; some things are passed
over in silence and remain unwritten. One must use this
"practical wisdom" given to us by God in our human logic,
to see *how* one should do *what*. He writes the following:

> But as for those things (in the Scripture) passed
> over in silence, the apostle Paul gives us a rule
> (κανόνα) which says "All things are lawful to me,
> but all things edify not. Let no man seek his own,
> but each his neighbor's good" (1 Cor 10:23). So
> that it is absolutely necessary, either to be subject to
> God according to his commandment (or scripture),
> or to others, i.e. to other commandments, because
> of his commandment.   (*Ascetic Works* 1)

In attempting to realize his leadership capacity, the
shepherd leads and cares in two ways according to Basil:
1. through prayers and the Eucharist and
2. by letters and visits (*Epistle 191*).

He says in his *Epistle 150,* that to him, after all, is
entrusted the οἰκονομία, the distribution of properties and
possessions to the poor, for his duty is to care not only for
the spiritual but also the bodily needs of his subjects. In
fact, this proper pastoral care makes the bodily needs a
spiritual matter. Not only is the shepherd responsible for
an orderly way to do this; he also is to "admonish offenders."
St Basil says that the leader does this first privately, then
in the presence of the Church, and if necessary, he must
eventually exclude the offender from the community. But
always, Basil says, one is to do this not to harm, but again,
only to lead the person to eventual repentance; even in
this, the shepherd is still a leader.

In both of these very exact functions, i.e. in prayer and
eucharist, then by letters and visits, Basil uses the metaphors
of eyes and lips to explain leadership. The eye of the body
discerns events, plans them, keeps watch on their development. The lips are there to communicate and to proclaim,
to confront and to teach (*Longer Interrogation 24*). He says
that the lips of the leader are there to write, in oral words,

"the words of eternal life on the hearts of the faithful" (*On Psalm 44:3*).

The other crucial issue which is integral to the shepherd as leader is preaching (κήρυγμα). This, however, will be reserved for the next major part of our study: the Ministry of the Word. However, for our present concern regarding the leader (*proestos*), we can conclude with St Basil's call for him to be a humble example to those entrusted to him by God:

> The leader, then, mindful of the apostle's injunction, "Be thou an example to them that believe" (1 Tim 4:12), must make his life a clear example of every commandment of the Lord, so as to leave the hearers no chance of thinking (it may be neglected). First of all then, which truly comes first, humility must be practiced by him in the love of Christ, that even when he is silent, the example of his deed (may speak). For if this is the standard of Christianity (i.e. according to the Incarnation of Christ), those who are entrusted with the guidance of many, ought by their own mediation to lead the weaker to the imitation of Christ, as the blessed Paul says: "Be ye imitators of me, even as I also am of Christ" (1 Cor 11:1).

CHAPTER FOUR

The Relations of Shepherd and Flock

1. Shepherding the Flock—St John Chrysostom

St John Chrysostom presents a voluminous amount of information regarding the ministry of the Church and particularly, of the shepherd. His best known and loved treatise on this subject is *On the Priesthood,* which is set in a "dialogue" with his friend Basil.

Because of the scope of his writing, it is necessary for us to set some parameters within all that is attributed to Chrysostom. In the end, we have decided on two of his foci:

1. the position of the shepherd himself, and
2. the behavior and obligations of the flock.

Together these constitute a total picture of the Church's ministry.

Lewis Patsavos gives us the idea for these parameters by stating that Chrysostom refers to both at once: the shepherd and the flock.

Chrysostom reminds us that the priest truly is an assignee of God, and instrument of Christ . . . In this way, he undertakes spiritual authority and becomes the shepherd of the flock. Out of this relationship arise the obligations of both shepherd and flock. Chrysostom constantly reminds the spiritual shepherd

of his accountability . . . (and) the flock is reminded
of its obligations to the spiritual shepherd.

Then Patsavos proceeds to explain just why Chrysostom
does deal with this entire range of shepherding.

In Chrysostom's second homily on 2 Timothy, we
read that the reason for all the misfortune in the
Church is the disruption of the harmonious relations
of the flock towards the spiritual shepherds. Esteem
and respect are no longer directed to them. Consequently, neither does it exist for God, since priests
are God's messengers. When, then, there is respect
for the shepherd, God too is honored in his person.[1]

With regard to Chrysostom, this section will deal only
with what could be discovered concerning the "harmonious
relations" in which the obligations of both shepherd and
flock are considered. Furthermore, our hope is to see how
these harmonious obligations are still a prime concern in
the ministry of the Church today. These two foci will lead
us to deal with more than his treatise *On the Priesthood,*
and secondly, they will direct us to some practical advice
to the flock. (Chrysostom deals much more with the flock
in relation to the shepherd than do either Basil or Gregory.)
In dealing with the shepherd himself, Chrysostom explores
two distinct areas: the *authority* of the shepherd, and the
shepherd's response in *pastoral crises.* In dealing with the
flock—the parish—he explores their behavior and obligation
in terms of faith and love, patience and suffering, and poverty
and wealth. He helps us, finally, to conclude our investigation
of his teachings by distinguishing between sheep and humans
in proper pastoral care.

The Authority of the Shepherd

The first thing that Chrysostom says about the authority
of the shepherd, takes the shape of the elevated honor of

[1]*Ibid.,* Patsavos, pp. 55-70.

his ministry; it is established through the Holy Spirit and is most evident in the liturgical rites.

> The work of the priesthood is done on earth, but it is ranked among heavenly ordinances. And this is only right, for no man, no angel, no archangel, no other created power, but the Paraclete himself ordained this succession, and persuaded men, while still remaining in the flesh to represent the ministry of angels. The priest, therefore, must be as pure as if he were standing in heaven itself, in the midst of those powers.

Then Chrysostom quickly adds that the honor of this ministry, is not only given by the Spirit, but is also truly directed toward service: to "inflame the souls" of the flock through the sacrifice.

> The priest stands bringing down, not fire, but the Holy Spirit. And he offers prayer at length, not that some flame "lit from above may consume the offerings, but that grace" may fall on the sacrifice through that prayer, set alight the souls of all, and make them appear brighter than silver refined in the fire ... Anyone who considers how much it means to be able, in his humanity, still entangled in flesh and blood, to approach that blessed and immaculate Being, will see clearly how great is the honor which the grace of the Spirit has bestowed on priests. It is through them that this work is performed, and other work no less than this in its bearing upon our dignity and our salvation. For earth's inhabitants, having their life in this world, have been entrusted with the stewardship of heavenly things. (*On the Priesthood,* III, 4)

But this "power" is not only given in the liturgical rites; it extends to "binding and loosing," as Christ has promised. This is a power which not even the angels and archangels have, nor is it limited to the body (as with temporal rulers), but to the "soul itself."

Priests have received an authority which God has not given to angels or archangels. Not to them was it said, "What things soever ye shall bind on earth shall be bound also in heaven; and what things soever ye shall loose, shall be loosed." Those who are lords on earth have indeed the power to bind, but only men's bodies. But this binding touches the very soul and reaches through heaven. What priests do on earth, God ratifies above. The Master confirms the decisions of his slaves. Indeed he has given them nothing less than the whole authority of heaven. For he says, "Whose soever sins ye forgive, they are forgiven, and whose soever sins ye retain, they are retained." What authority could be greater than that? "The Father hath given all judgment unto the Son." But I see that the Son has placed it all in their hands.

(On the Priesthood, III, 5)

To this Chrysostom adds:

Again, if a king confers on one of his subjects the right to imprison and release again at will, that man is the envy and admiration of all. But . . . the priest has received from God an authority much greater than that, as heaven is more precious than earth and souls than bodies.   *(On the Priesthood,* III, 5)

In fact, it is because of this honor, that St John clearly addresses the flock, saying they should not forget that he is an instrument of God, and that God can work through him, even though he is hardly "worthy." He writes in his *Second Homily on Timothy 2-3:*

Do you not know what the priest is? He is an angel of the Lord. Are they his own words that he speaks? If you despise him, you do not despise him, but God who ordained him . . . If God does not work through him, then there is no baptism, nor communion in the mysteries, nor blessing; you are no longer Christians.

What then, you say, does God ordain all, even the unworthy? God does not ordain all, but he works through all, though they themselves be unworthy, that the people may be saved.   (NPNF, p. 481)

And in order to drive this point home, Chrysostom seems even to exaggerate:

For if God spoke, for the sake of the people, by an ass, and by Balaam, a most wicked man (Num 22), much more will be speak by the mouth of the priest. What indeed will not God do or say for our salvation? By whom does he not act? For if he worked through Judas and through those others who prophesied, people to whom he will say: "I never knew you; depart from me, you evildoers" (Mt 7:23), and if others "cast out devils," will he not much more work through his priests?   (NPNF, p. 482)

Indeed, as one can see in these few selections, Chrysostom sees the shepherd as being transparent of the Lord himself, that is, the priest is truly an "instrument of Christ."

The Shepherd in Pastoral Crises

This high honor of the priesthood, however, does not mean that the shepherd will not be tested; here Chrysostom speaks realistically and clearly to the contemporary situation in the Church. Indeed, the shepherd will have to struggle even to a greater degree because of that honor. This is especially true in those crises in which other persons may fail, but in which the shepherd cannot. We shall use here only one example: when the shepherd is confronted with insult from the flock. What shall he do? How shall he respond?

First, Chrysostom says, the shepherd must understand, must discern, must interpret, his own inner workings in light of what God wants from him, and not according to his first impulse of passion. This is precisely what is required when the shepherd today is faced with a crisis (insult being only one example of the many) in his ministry.

An excellent example of such a crisis in ministry can be seen in how Chrysostom says one must handle his *anger* and *resentment* as a response to insult; he must use it to fight only the devil and to correct oneself, and never direct it in order to hurt another (e.g. the parishioner) who has insulted him. In fact, he says if this behavior is required of the flock, how much more is it required of the shepherd who leads the flock?

> We have anger given us, not that we may commit acts of violence on our neighbors, but that we may correct those that are in sin... Anger is implanted in us as a sort of sting to make us gnash with our teeth against the devil, to make us vehement against him, not to set us in array against each other... Art thou prone to anger? Be so against thine own sins; chastise thy soul. Scourge thy conscience, be a severe judge, and be merciless in thy sentence against thine own sins. This is the way to turn anger to account. It was for this that God implanted it within us.   (NPNF, vol. XIII, p. 58)

Can the shepherd, when such a crisis comes, afford to get trapped in any of the extreme reactions that may be precipitated by such anger? Unlike some in today's world, Chrysostom claims that one can neither indiscriminately "let it all out," nor can he pretend it is not there. Rather, there is a proper time and a proper direction for this anger, and the spiritual maturity of the shepherd is tested thereby:

> Let us use the thing (anger) at its proper time. The proper time for anger is never where we move in our own quarrel... Stand not up in thine own quarrel, neither avenge thyself.
>   (NPNF, vol. II, p. 110)

And in another place,

And what is the unsuitable time (for anger)? When
we do so as avenging ourselves.

                                        (NPNF, vol. 10, p. 110)

What will happen to the character of the shepherd if,
in this crisis, the insult to him becomes a deep-seated resentment against the flock; it will fester within him, and he
will not only injure himself, but he will not be able to lead
and persuade his sheep. John says he cannot "retain it in his
mind," or it will "tear him up."

It is not said merely, forego wrath; but retain it not
in your mind: think not of it; part with all your re-
sentments; do away with the sore. For you suppose
that you are paying him back the injury; but you
are first tormenting yourself, and setting up your rage
as an executioner within you in every part, and
tearing up your own bowels.

                                        (NPNF, vol. 10, p. 473)

And to make it perfectly clear to the shepherd:

It is impossible for one who is out of temper ever
to persuade (others)!   (NPNF, vol. 11, p. 204)

But how, then, should the shepherd deal with this crisis
and those insults which the flock may throw against him?
Chrysostom says: with a proper "fear of God and a mature
measurement of spiritual priorities (for "to fall into hell is
far more grievous").

Has anyone insulted you?... consider before all
things the fear of God, and you soon will be mild and
gentle.   (NPNF, vol. 10, p. 512)

And he quickly adds:

But even if it be a galling thing to you to become
friends with him who has grieved you, to fall into

hell is far more grievous. And if you had set this
(galling thing) against that (hell), then you would
have known that to forgive is a much lighter thing.
(NPNF, vol. 10, p. 379)

There is only one way for the shepherd to respond when
this crisis occurs: by "forgetting," and then, by "forgiving,"
for,

The fire of our wrath is increased ten thousand times
by memory.   (NPNF, vol. 14, p. 19)

The question then remains: "How can the shepherd
lead," when through the tortures of his memory which seem
like the "fury of a never silent storm" within him, or like
the punishment of hell before its time, this shepherd loses
the "reasoning of his soul"? Chrysostom unflinchingly addresses the issue:

The angry man deserves ten thousand punishments,
voluntarily casting himself into the pit of destruc-
tion, and before the hell which is still to come, suffering punishment from this already, by bringing a
certain restless turmoil and a never silent storm of
fury through all the night and through all the day,
upon the reasonings of his soul.
(NPNF, vol. 14, p. 175)

And then,

We have no ground of defense when we remember
a wrong: For there is nothing more grievous than the
remembrance of injuries.
(NPNF, vol. 14, p. 262)

Finally, he warns the shepherd:

Let none of you revengefully imagine evil against his
brother in your heart; and "let none of you think of

his neighbor's malice." It is not said merely, forego
wrath; but retain it not in thy mind; think not of
it; part with all resentment; do away with the sore!
(NPNF, vol. 9, p. 473)

Of course, "not remembering" in a crisis such as this
must be complemented by a positive act, i.e. by "returning
evil with good." How else can the shepherd, remembering
the lesson of the Great Shepherd in whose ministry he now
serves, respond to the flock? In making this point, St John
uses the imagery of giving food to the one who has injured
us; the person (parishioner), seeing the shepherd's Christ-
like response, will be encouraged himself:

For certainly no one would have the heart to regard
a man continually as his enemy to whom he has given
meat and drink ... Thus, then, did he encourage the
man who has been wronged, but observe also how
he unites again the man who has done the wrong
to him who has been provoked ... For there is no
one so degraded and unfeeling as to be unwilling,
when he receives meat and drink, to become the
servant and friend of him who does this for him ...
(NPNF, vol. 9, p. 229)

Thus St John speaks to the shepherd, and thus we are
reminded *today* about the character of the shepherd's person,
which is always tested with the greatest force by both the
devil himself and his own inner passion, whenever a crisis
in his ministry arises. He is to look for the good and
virtuous, but wipe out from his mind the grievous, so that
he is not "consumed by wrath."

Let us wipe away all (trespasses against us) from our
minds; and if any good thing has been done to us
by him that has grieved us, let us only reckon that;
but if anything is grievous and hard to bear, let us
cast it forth and blot it out, so that not even a
vestige of it remains.   (NPNF, vol. 14, p. 142)

Therefore, in using these brief examples of both the shepherd's elevated honor and his pastoral obligation (for which we have used only one example, the crisis of insult, in order to describe that obligation), we can see how St John describes the person and character of the shepherd.[2]

The Behavior and Obligations of the Flock

It is now important to turn to the second focus, the flock itself, and their ministry, i.e. the ministry of the laity within the Church. What are their oblibations, and what then, is the difficulty which the shepherd has in leading them toward the fulfillment of those obligations?

First, regarding the flock, it is their *faith* which is a precondition to receiving the gifts of God. In their own faith they will not look to judging the shepherd's worthiness, for he "will not harm them, if they have faith," and since in any case, God's gifts are not conditioned upon any power the priest himself has. Again Chrysostom drives home his point by using liturgical imagery:

Reverence him, because every day he ministers to you, causes the scripture to be read ... prays for you, offers supplications for you ... Say not, he is unworthy. How does that affect the matter? Does he that is worthy bestow these great benefits on you of himself? By no means! Everything comes about because of your faith. Not even the righteous man can benefit you, if you lack faith, nor the unrighteous harm you, if you have faith. ... Is it the good life of the priest or his virtue which confers so much on you? The gifts that God bestows are not such as to be effects of the power of the priest. Everything springs from grace. The priest has but to open his mouth, but God it is who works all things. The priest

[2]Chrysostom has said much more than this regarding his person, but our choice of this material is well representative of the whole (a special study on Chrysostom's writings on the role of the shepherd probably deserves its own place!).

only performs the sign ... The offering is the same
whether it is offered by a common man or by Peter
or Paul. Christ gave the same thing to his disciples
which the priests now minister. One is not less than
the other, for it is not men who consecrate it, but
Christ himself who bestows sanctification. For as the
words which God spoke are the same which the
priest now utters, so is the offering the same, just as
the baptism which he gave. Thus the whole is a
matter of faith. (*Second Homily on 2 Timothy 4,*
based on NPNF, vol. 13, p. 483)

But, of course, St John, as a shepherd himself, speaks
of the most practical issues of Christian living to his own
flock. What is valuable for our study is that, as he does
this, he might well be speaking as a shepherd in our own
day (indeed, in any day or age). What does he say to his
flock which carries such importance in our own ministry?
What can the shepherd of today learn from Chrysostom?

In dealing with the behavior of the flock, Chrysostom
speaks of three issues which are relevant to the contemporary
ministry: Faith and Love, Patience and Suffering, and The
Poor and Wealthy.

Faith and Love. Regarding the faith (πίστις) of the
flock, St John says this is never to be "conditional." The
faithful, of course, are to be thankful when they have been
delivered from one thing or another, e.g. "a sick child" or
an "ailing spouse." However, their faith tells them that even
when their petitions are not answered, i.e. when they do not
"get what they want," still a thankfulness is required. Here
the faithful will remember that God knows, even better than
they themselves know, what they should or should not have.
There is always something more which we do not know
about ourselves, and it is at that point where a true faith
enters. Thus we flee to God in both "consolation and
desolation."

Regarding this, Chrysostom speaks as if he were delivering a homily to a typical community in the contemporary
world:

Even now I see many who, on becoming more prayerful when their child is ailing or their wife sick, enjoy
some alleviation of their trouble. But they must,
even when not obtaining this petition, nevertheless
continue giving thanks and glorifying God. This is
the part of faithful servants, this the part of those
who are prayerful and love God as they ought: to
fly to him not only when in consolation, but also in
desolation. . . . But when a person serves him only
in time of consolation, he does not give proof of
much love, nor does he love Christ purely.

(*Commentary on The Evangelist*, Hom 35, p. 350)

This kind of faith is nothing which can be comprehended
"rationally" or "cognitively"; indeed, what is "rational" is
to give thanks *only* when one receives something! But faith
causes one to submit to God even his rational understandings, informing him that, in any case, such rational capacity
is always limited. Chrysostom, when speaking of such matters,
speaks of rationality as "reasoning":

Therefore, since we know all these things, let us not
examine into the things of God by reasoning (alone)
and let us not submit divine things to the order
prevailing among us, nor subject them to the necessity of nature, but let us think of them all reverently,
believing as the Scriptures have said. He who is
curious and meddlesome gains no profit; in addition
to not finding what he seeks, he will pay the extreme
penalty. You have heard that he (God) begot him
(Christ); believe what you have heard, but do not seek
out "how"; and do not on this account deny the be-
getting. This would be part of utter senselessness.

(*Commentary on The Evangelist*, Hom 24, pp.
230-240)

Thus if the Christian has such "reasoning"—and he
surely does—it is to know his own limits! It is faith which
begins precisely at that limitation of reason, i.e. faith often
begins where human reason ends.

When speaking of love (ἀγάπη), Chrysostom reminds the flock about the Great Shepherd's binding of the love for God (which always comes first), and the love for the neighbor (which grows out of the love for God). "On these two commandments depend all the law and the prophets" (cf. St Matthew 22:37-40):

> Do you perceive that the love of God is interwoven with ours, like a kind of cord binding it together? That is why Christ at one time spoke of two commandments; at another, one. For it is not possible for him who is receptive to the love of God not to possess the other kind of love.
>
> (*Commentary on The Evangelist,* Hom 77, p. 325)

Then St John speaks directly about the flock's love for each other, even for those among the flock who have an "evil disposition" (who, after all, need "a greater care"), as well as those with "incurable diseases." Even if we cannot cure them, he says, we can still provide "some relief," and apply the remedy of "bearing another's burden." Here he is directly addressing their own (the laity's) ministry:

> ... let us take pains about the care of our souls and about showing love for one another. Let us not tear our members to pieces but, in proportion as we see that they have evil dispositions, let us give them greater care. I say this, for it often happens that we see many people with difficult or incurable diseases in their bodies, and we apply remedies unceasingly. What, to be sure, is worse than feet afflicted with gout and what worse than gouty hands? Shall we, therefore, amputate the limbs? By no means! On the contrary, we make every effort to afford them some relief, since we cannot cure the affliction.
>
> Let us do this also in the case of our brethren; even if they are incurably ill, let us continue applying remedies. And let us bear one another's burdens. In

this way we shall both observe the precept laid down by Christ and attain to the blessings promised, by the grace and mercy of our Lord Jesus Christ. Glory be to him and to the Father, together with the Holy Spirit, forever and ever. Amen.

(*Commentary on The Evangelist,* Hom 68, p. 242)

Chrysostom says we are to have this love because of what we have in common with the brethren. "We have nothing in common only with the devil." And since we are all created in the image of God, we share a "like nature" which we must respect in the other. To understand this is to see in the other, the person of Christ himself. Again, Chrysostom speaks of this matter as the shepherd of today might to his own flock:

And make me not this reply: "What matters it to me? I have nothing common with him." With the devil alone we have nothing in common, but with all men we have many things in common; for they partake of the same nature with us; they inhabit the same earth, and they are nourished with the same food; they have the same Lord; they have received the same laws, and are invited to the same blessings with ourselves. Let us not say then, that we have nothing in common with them; for this is satanic speech; a diabolical inhumanity. Therefore let us not give utterance to such words, but exhibit such a tender care as becomes brethren!

(*Covering the Statues,* Hom 1, v. 32)

Finally, John adds that to act in the spirit of this ministry of love and care, not according to mere rational understandings but according to faith, is to "act rightly."

Since, therefore, he [God] renders to every man according to his works; for this reason he both implanted within us a natural law, and afterwards gave us a written one, in order that he might de-

mand an account of sins, and that he might de-
those who act rightly. Let us then order our conduct
with the utmost care.

(*Concerning the Statues,* Hom 12, v. 15)

And again, we do such works not according to our
"knowledge," but because our faith leads us to "uprightness
of life and character."

Therefore, even when he says: "Now this is ever-
lasting life, that they may know thee, the only true
God," let us not think that the knowledge mentioned
is of itself sufficient for salvation for us! We also
need uprightness of life and character.

(*Commentary on The Evangelist,* Hom 31, p. 297)

Finally, St John adds the reminder that faith without
works—or without love in the form of action—is not enough,
i.e. "faith without works is dead."

Let us not, then, beloved, think that faith suffices for
our salvation. If we do not give evidence of purity
of life, but present ourselves clad in a garment unworthy of this blessed invitation, nothing will prevent
us also from enduring the same sufferings as that
wretched man.

(*Commentary on The Evangelist,* Hom 10, p. 102)

Patience and Suffering. For Chrysostom, patience (ὑπο-
μονή) comes simply from relating to the experience of
Christ himself. This is a virtue that the flock is to remember
when they face their own tribulations. Here Chrysostom
uses the imagery of our Lord before Annas and Caiphas,
and then Pilate. To have patience as this is to place one's
soul in a "calm harbour."

Patience is a wonderful virtue. It places the soul in
a calm harbour, as it were, sheltering it from the
billows and winds of evil. Christ has taught us this

virtue at all times, but especially now when he is
being subjected to trial and forcibly driven from one
place to another. I say this for, when brought before
Annas, he replied with great gentleness, and everything he said in answer to the attendant who struck
him was calculated to dispel the mist of his pride.
Moreover, when he went from there to Caiaphas, and
then to Pilate, spending the whole night in these
"trials," he demonstrated his meekness throughout.
(*Commentary on The Evangelist,* Hom 84, p. 417)

Even when the Christian is insulted, patience should be
had. In this way he is to imitate Christ, so that "if you are
not troubled, you are not insulted." It is not, then, the one
who is afflicted that suffers, but if he continues in his
patience, only those who *do* the afflicting suffer:

Let us also imitate him, for in this way we shall be
able to remain unharmed by every kind of insult. For
it is not the one who offered insult, but the weak
character who is troubled by insults, who makes the
scoffing effective and causes it to give pain. If you
are not troubled, you are not insulted. The pain of
such suffering comes, not from those who inflict it,
but from those who regard it as suffering. Why,
indeed, are you troubled about it at all? If you are
insulted unjustly you particularly ought not to grieve
at this, but rather to be sorry for the one who wronged
you. And if you have been justly affronted, you have
much less cause for complaint.
(*Commentary on The Evangelist,* Hom 83, p. 414)

Because the flock is "instructed by Christ" himself in
this virtue of patience, even death cannot threaten them.
In making this point, Chrysostom applies the ultimate
sign—death—to any of "the events which come upon us
unexpectedly."

Should any one, therefore, threaten you with death,

say to him, "I am instructed by Christ not to fear them which kill the body, but are not able to kill the soul." Or should he threaten you with the confiscation of your goods, say to him, "Naked came I out of my mother's womb, and naked shall I return thither. We brought nothing into this world; and it is certain we can carry nothing out." "And though you take me not, death will come and take me; and though you slay me not, yet the law of nature will presently interfere and bring the end." Therefore we should fear none of these things which are brought on us by the order of nature, but those which are engendered by our own evil will; for these bring forth our penalty!

(*Concerning the Statues,* Hom 6, v. 9, p. 10)

As these examples indicate, the flock is encouraged by the shepherd to use the model of Christ as their instructor in such matters of patience and suffering.

On the Poor and Wealth. Chrysostom makes it quite clear to his flock that pride is the problem which leads to sin. So it is true even when concerning wealth. It is not wealth in itself, nor poverty (of material goods) in itself which is the virtue, but to be "unassuming," and not to be "careless of that which is within." He speaks of these characteristics in his *Homilies on the Statues*:

But here, it is worthy of inquiry, for what reason he (St Paul) does not say, "Charge those who are rich in the present world, not to be rich; charge them to become poor; charge them to get rid of what they have"; but, "charge them, not to be high-minded" (1 Tim 6:18). For he knew that the root and foundation of riches is pride and that if any man understood how to be unassuming, he would not make much ado about the matter. (Hom 2, v. 14)

For they who spend all their endeavors upon the

decoration of their dwelling, rich as they are in out-
ward things, are careless of that which is within,
letting their soul abide desolate and squalid, and
full of cobwebs. But if they would be indifferent to
exterior things, and earnestly expend all their attention upon the mind, adoring this at all points; then
the soul of such men would be a resting place for
Christ. And having Christ for its inhabitant, what
could ever be more blessed? Would you be rich? Have
God for your friend, and you shall be richer than
all men!   (Hom 2, v. 17)

Finally Chrysostom says:

Wherefore let us not consider riches to be a great
good; for the great good is, not to possess money, but
to possess the fear of God and all manner of piety.
                                            (Hom. 2, v. 21)

However, St John knows that the internal disposition of
the faithful does not stand by itself; it needs the act, the
"works" of love. Consequently, he relates the problem of
wealth and the poor to concrete acts of almsgiving and
charity. In fact, if pride (the internal disposition) is present,
he says, the flock will only "hear others passing by in
moaning, and will not go to their aid," will even become
"annoyed" at the poor:

Let us act this way also with regard to almsgiving,
and let us take pity on our fellow men; let us not
neglect those wasted by hunger. For, is it not strange
behavior for us to take our place at table amid gaiety
and luxury, while we hear others passing through
the streets moaning, and do not go to the aid of anyone
who is moaning, but even become annoyed at him and
call him an imposter? What is it you are saying my
man? Does anyone devise a fraud for one loaf of
bread? Indeed, when you drive away the poor man
who comes to you, be mindful of who it is that will

be coming as a suppliant to God. "With what measure you measure," Scripture says, "it shall me measured to you." Think how he goes off after being rebuffed: head bent low, grieving, because, besides his poverty, he has also received the blow of your affront.

(*Commentary on The Evangelist*, Hom 11, pp. 334-345)

Finally, Chrysostom reminds the flock that they are to "minister" according to the piety and virtues which give birth to these possibilities (Faith and Love, Patience and Suffering, the Poor and Wealth); they are to do this because this is the way to salvation and a "lasting pleasure."

... for every thing belonging to this life is liable to damage, and is unable to afford us a lasting pleasure; but piety and the virtue of the soul is altogether the reverse of this.

(*Concerning the Statues*, Hom 16, v. 14)

Pastoral Care: Of Sheep and Humans

Having approached the ministry of the Church in terms of both the shepherd and the flock, we can now turn to the act whereby they meet: *in pastoral care*. The characteristics of Christian living to which we have just pointed, cannot and will not happen without confronting the difficulty that is involved while leading the flock toward such characteristics. Since this is a problem for every pastor today, it holds a special interest for us. For this reason, Chrysostom's entire treatise *On the Priesthood* should be read by every person interested in the ministry of the priesthood. We will focus here only on Book Two and its emphasis on the difficulty of pastoral care.[3]

In Book Two of *On the Priesthood*, Chrysostom begins by drawing on an analogy between the shepherd of *humans*

[3]All the quotes used here, therefore, can be found in St John Chrysostom, *On the Priesthood*, trans. Graham Neville (Crestwood, NY: St Vladimir's Seminary Press, 1984).

and the shepherd of *animals,* i.e. of sheep, literally. He makes reference to our Lord's question to St Peter: "Simon, son of John, do you love me?" (Jn 21:16). The response, after Peter answers three times, is "Feed my sheep." But the shepherd, in this case, has a much more difficult calling, because it is a "rational flock" (II. 2), and it is one for which Christ himself died. While the shepherd of sheep may lose some animals to "wolves and thieves," he can be pardoned. Not so for the shepherd of the "rational flock"! He is one who "risks a penalty not of money, but of his own soul for the loss of the sheep."[4]

But how shall he lose his sheep? And why is this flock more difficult to protect? Because there must be a watch against the "principalities, against powers, against the world rulers of this darkness, against the spiritual hosts of wickedness in the heavenly places."[5] These are the most difficult because they come forward from the "principalities" to which St Paul referred. Even worse, unlike the shepherd of the "irrational flock," these "enemies seek not only the entire flock, but the shepherd also!" "They do not leave the shepherd alone, but attack him all the more!"[6]

Chrysostom then reminds us that whereas the shepherd of sheep has "full power to compel the sheep to accept the treatment if they do not submit of their own accord," it is not this way for the shepherd of the human community.

> But human diseases in the first place are not easy for a man to see; for "no one knows the things of a man save the spirit of the man which is in him." How, then, can anyone provide the specific cure for a disease if he does not know its character and often cannot tell whether the man is ill at all?
>
> (*On the Priesthood,* II. 2)

St John elaborates on this particular difficulty of pastoral care by stating that, even if the shepherd could discern the

[4]*On the Priesthood,* p. 54
[5]*Ibid.*
[6]*Ibid.,* p. 55.

infirmity, he still cannot "doctor" his flock as the shepherd of the sheep. This is true because of the very nature of the "rational man." Being born in God's image and thereby being given free-will, it is *his* will which is as much involved as the shepherd's: "For the man does not exist who can by compulsion cure someone else against his will."[7]

Furthermore, the shepherd must consider the fact that force cannot be used.

> For Christians above all men are forbidden to correct the stumblings of sinners by force. When secular judges convict wrong-doers under the law, they show that their authority is complete and compel men, whether they will or no, to submit to their methods. But in the case we are considering it is necessary to make a man better not by force but by persuasion.
> *(On the Priesthood,* II. 2)

In all this, St John knows that these conditions have always been—and will continue to be—a difficulty for the pastor-as-shepherd. How does the shepherd "persuade" the flock? How does he lead them to accept "treatment"? Chrysostom says good judgment is required:

> For this reason a lot of tact is needed, so that the sick many be persuaded of their own accord to submit to the treatment of the priests, and not only that, but be grateful to them for their cure. *(On the Priesthood,* II. 2)

Himself asking, "what then should you do?" Chrysostom proceeds to offer the shepherd some eternal wisdom regarding pastoral care. Discretion is an obvious ingredient for Chrysostom, because if the shepherd's words of admonition are too lenient, he then becomes like the surgeon who fails to make a deep-enough incision, thus "mutilate yet miss the cancer." If, on the other hand, the incision is made without careful discretion and sensitivity, the patient will

[7]*Ibid.,* p. 57.

throw everything away at once, "medicine and bandage alike, and promptly throw himself over a cliff." Needless to say, such balance in "dealing with the wrongs of the flock," is a most difficult challenge for the shepherd; being wrongly too lenient or too rigid and unbending only leads the parishioner to a fall into despair. Chrysostom finally makes this point directly:

> It is not right simply to exact a penalty by the measure of the sins; some guess must be made about the disposition of the sinner. (*On the Priesthood,* II. 3)

The shepherd, therefore, needs to be "self-disciplined" (although he claims, not only this!—for "the man who practices asceticism helps no one but himself") and a "wise servant" at the same time; this is needed for the proper "pastoral function" which is "extended to the whole people." Knowing fully that it is not possible for anyone to cure a man by compulsion against his will, this shepherd will:

> keep on thinking and saying:... God may give them the knowledge of the truth and they may be freed from the snare of the devil. (*On the Priesthood,* II. 4)

Thus, St John Chrysostom presents a most complete picture of the difficulty of pastoral care, one which clearly involves the total commitment of the shepherd who shall answer to Christ that indeed he loves Christ's sheep and will in all ways possible "feed them"; and of the flock who must, out of respect and love for God himself, even so respect and love their shepherd who seeks to lead them.

2. Other Fathers on the Nature of Shepherding

Besides the Three Hierarchs, there are other Fathers who address pastoral issues which center around our concern for the ministry. Some of these Church Fathers serve well to close this chapter on the ministry of the Church.

Of the Latin Fathers, Sts Augustine, Ambrose, and
Gregory the Great speak of the shepherd.

St Augustine, bishop of Hippo from 395 to 430, in
writing to Honoratus (another bishop), explains the implications of fleeing from the cruel persecutions of the
Donatists. Augustine gives valuable insight into the duty
of the shepherd, whose first responsibility is to minister to
his people. Although there are certain circumstances in which
the shepherd, being "personally sought out," may flee "into
fortified places," there is to be no "shirking of the duties
of his ministry." He is to do this because otherwise there
would be no Church, nor Christians. Thus the shepherd can
flee "so long as the Church is not abandoned by others who
are not thus pursued."

> I wrote in that letter . . . let the servants of Christ, the
> ministers of his word and of his sacrament, do what
> he has commanded or permitted. Let them by all
> means flee from city to city when any one of them
> is personally sought out by persecution, so long as the
> Church is not abandoned by others who are not thus
> pursued, and who may furnish nourishment to their
> fellow-servants, knowing that otherwise these could
> not live.

> But when the danger is common to all, that is, to
> bishops, clerics, and laity, those who depend upon
> others are not to be forsaken by those on whom they
> depend. Therefore, either all should move to places
> of refuge, or those who have to stay should not be
> abandoned by those who should minister to their
> spiritual needs . . . The man who is to escape the
> horrors of invasion, but who does not flee because he
> will not forsake the ministry of Christ (without which
> men can neither become nor live as Christians), wins
> a greater reward for his charity than the one who
> flees for his own sake, not for his brethren, but who

is caught, refuses to deny Christ, and wins martyrdom.[8]

St Ambrose, who was elected to the episcopacy in 374
and preached often on the subject of the pastoral ministry
of the shepherd until his death in 397, addressed his flock
at Milan with these words:

> The duty of the priest or minister is to help all, if
> it is posible, and to harm no one. Therefore, if an-
> other cannot be helped without being hurt, it is better
> not to help him so as not to hurt him. And therefore
> the priest should not intervene in monetary matters
> in which it is often impossible not to hurt the one
> who loses, because he thinks that he has lost through
> the good work of the intercessor. It belongs to the
> priestly office to do harm to no one and to be desirous
> of helping everyone; but the accomplishment of this
> can come only from God.[9]

And in another place St Ambrose speaks of the virtues
of the priest. In this regard, it is true that the shepherd, who
stands also before "those outside the flock," i.e. "in the
public eye," should behave in a manner worthy of respect.

> Thus, in St Paul's qualifications for the ministry, we
> see how many qualities are asked of us: that the
> minister of the Lord should refrain from the use of
> wine, and be safeguarded by the good testimony not
> only of the faithful but also of those outside the fold.
> It is fitting that the public eye should be witness of
> our acts and works lest it lose respect for our office;
> in order that whoever sees the minister of the altar
> adorned with fitting virtues should give glory to their
> author and honor the master who has such servants.[10]

St Gregory the Great, who was a monk before he became

[8]*The Fathers of the Church,* Letter 228, pp. 141-143, ed. Defarri,
New York.
[9]*Ibid.,* P.L. Duties of Ministers, 3, 9, pp. 58-59.
[10]*Ibid.,* P.L., 6, p. 103ff.

pope in 500, writes in his *Pastoral Rule* (written after his election to this rank), that the shepherd of souls must be "pure in thought," or this pollution will pollute others. This happens since "the hand that would cleanse dirt must needs be clean."

> The ruler (of souls) should always be pure in thought, inasmuch as no impurity ought to pollute him who has undertaken the office of wiping away the stains of pollution in the hearts of others also; for the hand that would cleanse from dirt must needs be clean, lest, being itself sordid with clinging mire, it soil whatever it touches all the more.[11]

In another passage of the same *Pastoral Rule,* the shepherd must be "chief in action," since the "flock, which follows the voice and manners of the shepherd" needs the example even more than the words; "to speak" must never be separated from "to exist."

> The ruler (of souls) should always be chief in action, that by his living he may point out the way of life to those that are put under him, and that the flock, which follows the voice and manners of the shepherd, may learn how to walk better through example than through words. For he who is required by the necessity of his position to speak the highest things, is compelled by the same necessity to exhibit the highest things. For that voice more readily penetrates the hearer's heart, which the speaker's life commends, since what he commands by speaking, he helps the doing of by showing.[12]

In the East, the Greek Fathers (with the exception of the three Hierarchs) who speak of the shepherd are Sts Ephraim the Syrian, Dionysios, Gregory of Nyssa, and Cyril of Alexandria.

[11]*Ibid.,* P.L., Reg. Past., II cap. 2, 77, 27.
[12]Loc. cit., cap. 3.

St Ephraim the Syrian writes that the shepherd must endeavor to be like those Old Testament examples:

> And remember, my beloved, that I wrote to you concerning the fathers of old, that they first learned the ways of tending sheep and, in that, received the trial of carefulness; then they were chosen for the office of guides, that they might learn and observe how much the pastor cares for his flock . . . Thus Joseph was chosen . . . and Moses was chosen . . . and David . . . and Amos . . . and Elisha.

Then Ephraim adds:

> O ye pastors, be made like unto that diligent pastor, chief of the whole flock, who cared so greatly for his flock. He brought nigh those that were afar off. He brought back the wanderers. He visited the sick. He strengthened the weak. He bound up the broken. He guarded the fatlings. He gave himself up for the sake of the sheep.[13]

Dionysios, the unknown mystical author at the end of the fifth century, writes of the "divinity" of the priest's position within his famous "sacred hierarchy."

> Everyone constituted in the sacred hierarchy, according to his position and the nature of his orders, is initiated into divine things and divinized, so that he may impart to those who come after him, a share of this divinization which he has received from God.[14]

And in another place, Dionysios claims that as the shepherd has been given the share of "divinity," this task is now to lead each of the flock into "the imitation of God according to his capacity." In this way each one is a "fellow-worker

---

[13]"Of Pastors" in *Nicene Post-Nicene Fathers* (Eerdmans, Grand Rapids, Mich.), vol. XIII, pp. 384-385.

[14]*Ibid.*, P.G., The Ecclesiastical Hierarchy, pp. 372-373.

with God," and a "reflection of the divine operation." Of course, since each member of the flock is different and it is the shepherd's distinct task to guide each one, precisely "according to his capacity" and "to the best of his ability," here enters the shepherd's capacity to "discern" and to help in developing the gifts (*charismata*) which each has received from God.

St Gregory of Nyssa (†394), noting how the Holy Spirit causes external and physical substances (such as the bread in the Holy Eucharist) to produce internal and spiritual effects, uses the same reasoning in regard to priestly consecration.

> The selfsame power of the word makes the priest holy and venerable, for he is "set apart" from the rest of the community by the new blessing which he has received. Though but yesterday he was one of many, one of the people, now he is suddenly proclaimed a leader, a ruler, a teacher of piety, a priest of hidden mysteries. And this comes about without any change at all in his bodily appearance. As far as externals go, he is who he was; but his invisible soul is changed for the better by a certain invisible power and grace.[15]

Finally, St Cyril of Alexandria summarizes our original thesis, that the shepherd serves in the ministry of the Lord Jesus himself, and that it is that Great Shepherd who ordains this shepherd by the Holy Spirit. St Cyril says:

> Our Lord Jesus Christ ordained [the disciples] pastors and teachers of the whole world and ministers of his divine mysteries . . . And when he had said this, he breathed on them, and said to them, "Receive the Holy Spirit . . ." After elevating them to a position of eminence by the great dignity of the apostolate, and appointing them priests and ministers at the altars of

[15]Ibid., P.G., *Sermon on the Baptism of Christ*, pp. 581-584.

God, he at once sanctifies them, breathing upon them openly and giving them his Spirit. He shows that it is necessary for the Spirit to be given to those whom he chooses for the divine apostolate ... because they can do nothing pleasing to God, nor can they free themselves from the chains of sin, unless they are first clothed with power from on high and changed into something other than they were ... And Paul, that wisest of men, after remarking that he had labored more than others in the apostolate, added at once "though it was not I but the grace of God which is with me" (1 Cor 15:10). ... Our Lord Jesus Christ ... brings to perfection priests for the altar of God, and he does this by sanctifying them in very truth, making them share in his own nature by communication of the Spirit, and in a manner fusing the nature of man with a power and glory which is more than human.[16]

---

[16]*P.G.* Commentary on St John, 7-8, p. 712.

PART II

THE MINISTRY OF THE WORD

"Follow the pattern of the sound words ... in the faith and love which are in Christ Jesus; guard the truth that has been entrusted to you by the Holy Spirit who dwells within us."

(2 Tim 1:13-14)

"But we will give ourselves continuously to prayer and to the ministry of the word."

(Acts 6:4)

CHAPTER FIVE

Preaching in the Scriptures
and the Fathers

1. Preaching: A "Strange Thing"

"Familiarity makes us miss the wonder of a strange thing that happens every Sunday."[1] The Ministry of the Word, which is fulfilled in the gift of the Holy Spirit, occurs to our limited human minds as a "strange thing." How is this so?

Each Sunday, Christian engineers, students, children, white-collar and blue-collar workers leave behind the usual affairs of the week and come from their homes to the church in order to experience this movement of the Holy Spirit in their lives. This event each week seems "strange," first of all, in relation to the words and activity of their "everyday" world. And yet, when they come to the church with the proper spiritual attitude, it is because they truly expect to make a special contact with the Almighty God. The Ministry of the Word is part of that special contact.

There has never been anything else as romantic in all the adventure stories of the human race. The quest for the Holy Grail and the Argonaut's search for the Golden Fleece becomes common-place in comparison

[1]George Sweazey, *Preaching the Good News* (Englewood Cliffs, N.J.: Prentice-Hall, 1976) p. 40. It should also be said that much of this chapter was presented in a different form during the "Liturgical and Pastoral Institute" at St Vladimir's Orthodox Seminary, June, 1982.

with this weekly event. But do these seekers find what they are looking for? If not, theirs is a peculiarly persistent mistake, with fifty-two chances a year to find out that the encounter with God does not occur.[2]

The "strange thing," of course, is not exhausted by this Ministry of the Word; rather, this particular ministry is a central part of this larger encounter with God—and that experience can never be limited to fifty-two times a year.

This "strange thing" is a veritable "miracle" in terms of the word which is spoken. Every student who has studied theology in preparation for the ministry of the priesthood knows this. One goes to his assigned parish and is greeted by persons who, just the year before, could have been teaching him about those certain subjects included now in his preaching. But these persons are there, every Sunday at least—and hardly because they expect to "learn" some new information, the sort of which they can find in their well-stocked home libraries. What can that young pastor think, as he preaches to them? What, he wonders, is really happening here? Obviously, he knows that this is no simple "lesson"—although a lesson is part of it.

What he does soon learn, is that whatever it is that happens, it does not happen *because* of himself, but *in spite of* himself! It is a miracle in the sense that what does happen is not utterly explainable according to the criteria of our everyday judgments; an event happens in this Ministry of the Word which is not caused by an earthly effort alone!

This miracle is the preacher's only hope. Could anyone expect to be able to do what [he] is supposed to do—to introduce people to Jesus Christ, to persuade them to accept the Christian Faith, to show people how to live as Christians, to comfort, strengthen, inspire? [This claim] would make a field marshal blush![3]

The fact that this event—this "strange thing" which

2Loc. cit., Sweazey.
3Ibid., Sweazey, p. 40.

happens—is comprised of such "persuading," "showing," "living," "comforting," "reproving," "strengthening," "inspiring," and perhaps more, means only that it is a true *ministry,* since as we have already established, ministry means *serving.*

It is no less a ministry, and certainly no less a mysterious ministry, than when the pastor finds himself faced with a tragedy in the life of his parishioners. Who does not recall that time when, perhaps because a child has suddenly died, this pastor drags himself up to the door, rings the doorbell, and wonders what, in God's name, he is going to say to these parents. When he enters and finally speaks, it is almost not himself who is uttering these words—and yet, indeed, it is his very voice. That "strange thing" happens again.

As he leaves, he may even feel he has failed, that the words perhaps did not "carry," that perhaps they did not radiate the strength and comfort he hoped would be given. Even then, he is not sure of what words were exactly spoken.

And yet, he might be fortunate enough that some day later the phone will ring: "Father, your coming was just what we needed. It reminded us of what our life and faith truly is. It told us what we can hope, and even, how we can go on living." And in response, does not that young priest wonder in astonishment, "who me?" Again, it is that "strange thing."

But the point is that the answer of that "strange thing" in each case is, "no, not you." At least not you alone. There is something more than human which has happened. One certainly cooperates with it, makes himself an instrument of it, prepares himself as best he can in order to be a channel for it—but in the end, he knows that this event remains the "strange thing," a mixture of himself and of the Spirit given by God. It is, to be sure, a mystery which has happened, but it is not vague, nor is it ever humanless.

Our effort in this chapter will be to unfold this Ministry of the Word, which has deep meaning for both clergy and laity since it involves the task of both ministries to which we have already alluded. This we will do, with the knowl-

edge that as we proceed, the "strange thing" will always
be operative, always engaging, always lifting up our own
human part in this ministry.

We also must not forget that what Christ promised
us will continue to be with us: "It is not you who speak,
but the Holy Spirit" (Mk 13:11). Or again, "I will give
you a mouth and wisdom which none ... will be able to
withstand" (Lk 21:15). We also will not forget what
St. Paul said: "We impart this in words, not taught by
human wisdom, but taught by the Spirit" (1 Cor 2:13).
It is, thus, *God's presence* through Christ and the Holy
Spirit, along *with* the one who preaches, that comprises
the "strange thing" that happens. "My presence will go
with you." This, God promised the frightened Moses,
who was himself called to lead and minister to his people. And Moses' reply is our very own: "If thy presence will not go with me, do not carry us up from here"
(Ex 33:14-15).

2. Early Christian Roots of the Ministry of Preaching

In an earlier chapter on the apostolic ministry, St Paul
was by-passed for the sake of establishing the proper foundation in this section on the Ministry of the Word, for Paul
is totally identified with our present task of preaching:

> The Apostle about whom we knew the most—and
> whose function of preaching has devolved upon to-
> day's priests—is the missionary Apostle Paul. For
> Paul, "a laterborn Apostle," was an instrument chosen
> by God to preach the Gospel.[4]

St Paul preached the very same Gospel which St Peter
and the other apostles (and their followers) preached. Indeed, Paul knew himself to be precisely one of these apostles,
and found his very existence within the same task of proclaiming the great works of Christ.

[4]Edward P. Echlin, *The Priest as Preacher: Past and Future* (Notre-Dame:
Fides) p. 15.

But he who had set me apart before I was born, and
had called me through his grace, was pleased to
reveal his Son in me, in order that I might preach
him among the Gentiles ... And they glorified God
because of me.   (Gal 1:15-16,24)

Christ is revealed in St Paul, and then Paul preaches
out of the very person of Christ. He first "receives" this
ministry of the word which is delivered to him, and then
he delivers it to others.

For I delivered to you as of first importance what I
also received, that Christ died for our sins in ac-
cordance with the scriptures, that he was buried, that
he was raised on the third day ... that he appeared
to Cephas, then to the twelve, ... to more than five
hundred brethren ... to James ... to all the Apostles.
Last of all, as to one untimely born, he appeared
also to me.   (1 Cor 15:3-8)

It is only, in fact, what he has "received" and then
"delivered," which makes him an apostle, although he is
"unfit to be called an apostle, because I persecuted the
church of God" (1 Cor 15:9). In short, he is a collaborator
of all those, both before and after him (and even in some
sense, in the Old as well as in the New Testament), who
have preached and will preach this very same word: "Whether
then it was I or they, so we preach and so you believed"
(1 Cor 15:11). The message—its essence and reason—is
always the same, although as we shall soon see, it must be
applied and delivered differently.

The one who preaches today is rooted precisely in this
continuous ministry of the word; his own speech is in col-
laboration with the community of those who rightly preached,
before and after him, and with the power of God.

The question is: what part does God play and does man
play in the proclamation of the Word? Some imply that God
does it all, man having no great input. Others imply that
the entire effort can be reduced to mere human "techniques."

Both are wrong, and it is to a proper dynamic, a proper "synergy" of Divine presence in human speech (and here St Paul truly stands as an excellent model) that we must immediately turn. The "strange thing" that happens in the homiletic event, as indicated earlier, needs such a Divine-human synthesis.

Regarding this proper dynamic, both St Paul, as well as the others who continue in this very same ministry, do not preach in isolation from a certain community experience and foundation, both culturally and otherwise. Before we look more carefully at St Paul as our model *par excellence,* we must briefly take note of such formative roots in preaching the word.

3. The Divine-Human Dynamic in the Community

Obviously, although there are no formal rules for preaching in the Scripture, there are some influential characteristics which appear in biblical history and condition the one who preaches. In the early Church, the twin sources are the *biblical* and the *classical* forms of rhetoric.

> The Bible gives the motive, content and inspiration for Christian preaching, while forms and rules for effective public discourse come from the highly developed Greek and Roman rhetoric [theory] and oratory [practice] of the ancient world.[5]

The words Our Lord Jesus Christ spoke in the Gospel of St Matthew seem to have already been known in the Hebrew culture:

> I tell you, on the day of judgment men will render account for every careless word they utter; for by your words you will be justified and by your words you will be condemned.   (Mt 12:36-37)

[5]Craig Skinner, *The Teaching Ministry of the Pulpit* (Grand Rapids, Michigan: Baker Book House, 1973) p. 20.

To be "justified" or "condemned" by the words which are spoken, points to the central importance of human speech and right language. The Hebrew community knew this, and the exacting work of the scribes and prophets whose purpose rested upon a close attention to "textual demands," seems to emphasize this:

> The great strophes of the prophetic records, particularly those of Isaiah and Jeremiah, show an intimate acquaintance with the majesty and power of "right language." There is deep drama and biting force in almost every line of the originals. These men knew how to make their messages live for their hearers through apt illustration and telling metaphor. Their competence in these areas [points to] the probability of literary studies in such teaching communities as the "schools of the prophets."[6]

The concept of "schools of prophets," not as an institution as such, but precisely as an idea that proceeds from the "teaching community" (a community a person could learn from, and preach out of, i.e. the community experience as lived in a proper relationship with God) is crucial to grasp in terms of the significance of human speech.

In fact, the centrality of this upright and moral rhetoric is caught in the Scripture itself, for example in Ecclesiastes:

> Besides being wise, the Preacher also taught the people knowledge, weighing, studying and arranging proverbs with great care. The Preacher sought to find pleasing words and uprightly he wrote words of truth.   (Ecc 12:9-10)

It is not, as some might be tempted to think, merely because such a rhetoric stands by itself, as in some form of "art," or even as a sort of "deception" ("Oh, that's only rhetoric!") but only because of its final purpose:

[6]*Ibid.*, p. 21.

The end of the matter: Fear God, and keep his commandments; for this is the whole duty of man.
(Ecc 12:13)

This follows the quotation which shows that the words
and their final purpose, i.e. the rhetoric and its ultimate
meaning, are both important in the preaching task:

The sayings of the wise are like goads, and like
nails firmly fixed are the collected sayings which are
given by one Shepherd.   (Ecc 12:11)

Thus, the power of the "right word" is deeply known
and appreciated by those who inherit the task of preaching
the New Covenant: "a word fitly spoken is like apples
of gold in a setting of silver" (Prov 25:11). In fact, the
entire book of Proverbs, whose purpose is to transmit "wisdom and instruction" (1:2) to the Hebrew community,
speaks of its aim precisely in such terms as "right word"
and "final purpose."

That men may know wisdom and instruction, understand words of insight, receive instruction in wise
dealings, righteousness, justice, and equity; that
prudence may be given to the simple, knowledge and
discretion to the youth ... to understand a proverb,
and a figure, the words of the wise and their riddles.
(Prov 1:2-6)

And the purpose, as finally summarized, is this:

The fear of the Lord is the beginning of knowledge;
fools despise wisdom and instruction.   (Prov 1:7)

Turning to the New Testament, the apostles and disciples
focus their words on the meaning of one statement: "Jesus
is the Lord." If there was a temptation to preach this fact
with "oratorical trickery," then St Paul was certainly aware
of it; again an upright rhetoric was his rule:

> And my speech and my message were not in plausible
> words of wisdom but in demonstration of the Spirit
> and power.				(1 Cor 2:4)

Paul's speech and preaching which "demonstrates the
Spirit and power" were clearly words that came from his
own mouth; he himself is involved in them. They were not
spoken recklessly or carelessly, not taken lightly, nor used
as mere human and enticing words; they were direct and
concise. That his human effort was involved does not mean
that they were less than a full "demonstration of the Spirit
and power." In fact, there are clearly those times when it
was necessary to so "demonstrate the Spirit and power" in
a very careful and controlled human expression: "The style
of his Athenian address is faultless, and shows evidence of
most careful and controlled expression"[7] (cf. Acts 17:22-33).

No preacher today should then pretend that one preaching "by the Spirit and power" has himself no important
part in such a "demonstration"; he cannot simply "say what
he pleases," in a careless manner, with no effort or with
no training in its various forms. Nor should he pretend that
the homiletic task does not take his own human planning in
cooperation with the Holy Spirit; prayer, study—the planning
itself—is a form of cooperation with the Spirit. Although
this is different for different persons, it is nevertheless true
that in terms of preaching God's Word, to fail to plan is
to plan to fail! Today this may include everything from a
proper theological education to one's own personal preparation before the homily is to be delivered.

St Paul knows this truth and says so in his second letter
to Timothy:

> Follow the pattern of the sound words which you have
> heard from me, in the faith and love which are in
> Christ Jesus.				(2 Tim 1:13)

It is clear: "learning" is crucial to St Paul. One finds
the constant endorsement of proper instruction in terms of

[7]*Ibid.,* p. 22.

upright and careful speech; he knows that good preaching does not exist without the person's preparation and input, even though when the preaching event happens, it becomes more than what he humanly says. This is how one like Alexander Elchaninov preached: he always prepared *what* he was going to preach, although not *how*.[8] Regarding this very point, St Paul writes to Timothy:

> Do your best to present yourself to God as one approved, a work-man who has no need to be ashamed, rightly handling the word of truth. Avoid such godless chatter, for it will lead people in more and more godlessness.   (2 Tim 2:15-16)

and earlier:

> And what you have heard from me before many witnesses, entrust to faithful men, who will be able to teach others also.   (2 Tim 2:2)

St Paul also makes this same point in 1 Timothy, when he says that the "bishop" must be "an apt teacher" (1 Tim 3:2), that he should "attend to the public reading of scripture, to preaching, to teaching" (1 Tim 4:13), and that they are to be considered worthy of double honor who "labor in preaching and teaching" (1 Tim 5:17).

Such importance given to the Divine-human synergy in the ministry of the word, then, extends from the Hebrew community, through the apostolic age, and into the age of patristic preaching.

As was previously mentioned, the biblical and classical impulses continue to work in the patristic preaching. A cursory reading of their history shows that, from Origen on, through both the Greek and Latin Fathers, they had an ab-solute fidelity to biblical verse and meaning, and then used their "secular" education to practically apply it.[9] Regarding that education,

[8]Alexander Elchaninov, *The Diary of a Russian Priest* (Crestwood, NY: St Vladimir's Seminary Press, 1982) p. 19 and p. 220.
[9]Dietrich Ritschl, *A Theology of Preaching* (Richmond, Va.: John

In that ancient world the seven "liberal arts" of education were generally listed in the order of grammar, dialectic (logic) and rhetoric, as a primary group. The group (most emphasized in our contemporary education) was quite secondary to these three, usually listed as arithmetic, geometry, astrology and music. Thus there was an emphasis on the humanities and literary skills, and this emphasis held educational sway in the first five centuries of the Christian era. Within this emphasis, rhetoric was principal.[10]

Thus an educated man who preached had mastered the construction and delivery of a secular discourse through his general education, and then brought this training to bear upon the eternal word of God. This is true, even though they were always cautious to distinguish the mode from the content, being constantly concerned with the possible "creeping in" of philosophic presuppositions—or as St Paul warned, "the persuasive words of man's wisdom."

These Fathers, then, were indeed careful but also creative, in matching (actually submitting) the rules of rhetoric to the attitude of a proper spirituality. St Augustine, in his *On Christian Teaching,* not only deals with the priest's personal life and attitudes (as being dependent upon the Holy Spirit), but with the application of human training and speech.

Two great summations still stand as abridgements of St Augustine's thought having contemporary value. About the preacher's objectives he said, *"Non solum docere ut unstruat, et delectare ut teneat, verum etiam flectere ut vincat"* ("Not only to teach that he may instruct him, and to please that he may hold him, but also to move that he may overcome him.") About the relevance of style to the subjects discussed, he advised, *parva submisse, modica temperate, magna graditer"*

Knox Press) and Roy Pearson, *The Ministry of Preaching* (New York: Harper, 1959).

[10]*Ibid.,* Skinner, *The Teaching Ministry,* p. 24.

("Little things humbly, ordinary things moderately, great things grandly").[11]

Thus one can see, from the Old Testament through our own time, this ministry of the word is realized through a true Divine-human dynamic: God, as "the One Shepherd," has given these words as gifts to us, that through our "struggle" with them (and in truth, through our sweat and effort to transform them) we may give them distinct and purposeful human form, thereby transmitting them to others (Ecc 12:11). In this way rhetoric as the "right word," with the true, ultimate and final meaning of those words, is realized through human cooperation with God himself, who lifts this process up and gives it its efficacy. Together, they offer to the world the way to faith and true life.

This, of course, is precisely what the Evangelists did: each spoke his words, or rather, The Word, through his gospel; it is the very same Gospel, and yet each spoke it differently, according to his purpose. Thus, in the proclamation of the Word, we are evangelists.

4. St Paul: A Model of the Preacher

We can now turn directly to our chosen model, St Paul. Having established these factors of the Divine-human co-operation in the ministry of the word, we have already glimpsed a bit of St Paul's roots as a preacher. But there is more to be discovered about the great apostle and his ministry of preaching.

Paul felt that it was his preaching which identified him as an apostle. Throughout his epistles he appears to preach out of an assimilation to God, much the same as Ezekiel who "consumes the word" which is written on a scroll.

And he said to me, "Son of man, ... eat this scroll, and go, speak to the house of Israel." So I opened my mouth, and he gave me the scroll to eat.

(Ezek 3:1-2)

[11]Ibid., Skinner, *The Teaching Ministry*, p. 27.

This deep unity with and assimilation to God, in which Paul calls himself "a servant of God and an apostle of Jesus Christ" (Ti 1:1), in which he even claims "it is no longer I who live, but Christ who lives in me" (Gal 2:20), shows us that he truly believed that his proclamation was not disconnected from the example of life toward which he himself struggled. He knows that he has never "arrived" at a point when he ceases to struggle, but he invites others, through his preaching, to join in this very same struggle of his. Can less be said of the task today?

This preaching was committed to St Paul—God's manifested Word which was "promised before the world began":

In the hope of eternal life, which God who cannot lie, promised us before the world began: But has in due time manifested his word through preaching; which is committed unto me, according to the commandment of God our Savior.   (Ti 1:2-3 KJV)

So significant is this preaching to his identity as an apostle, that even if he could not remember who he baptized, he could never forget to whom he preached. This means that, although Paul certainly included himself in the sacramental life of the early Church (e.g. "the cup of blessing which we bless ... the bread which we break ..." (1 Cor 10:16), he nevertheless emphasizes—sometimes to the extreme—the centrality of the preaching:

I am thankful that I baptized none of you except Crispus and Gaius; ... (I did baptize also the household of Stephanas. Beyond that, I do not know whether I baptized any one else.) For Christ did not send me to baptize, but to preach the Gospel.
(1 Cor 1:14 and 16-17)

As an apostle committed to this ministry of the word, Paul believed that he was to be a "full-time" apostle, i.e. that this ministry should not be—although in a sense it necessarily was for Paul—a part-time ministry. In this respect

St Paul felt he deserved the financial support of the community, as well as some of the other "rights" of the apostles:

> Do we not have the right to our food and drink? Do we not have the right to be accompanied by a wife, as the other apostles and the brothers of the Lord and Cephas? Or is it only Barnabas and I who have no right to refrain from working for a living. Who serves as a soldier at his own expense? Who plants a vineyard without eating any of its fruit? Who tends a flock without getting some of the milk?
> (1 Cor 9:4-7)

From this we can see how important, how absolutely crucial to St Paul, is this ministry of the word. This is the central message for all that follows regarding this particular ministry.

For St Paul, the proclamation of the Word is also "ministry" that takes particular "forms." What kind of forms?

First, St Paul spoke to at least seven different communities, and he addressed each community according to its distinct situation and circumstance, while proclaiming one basic message. St Paul preached to these communities as a pastor who is interested in "building up the One Body" as it engages that particular circumstance. His basic message is "oneness"; they are baptized into this One Body:

> For just as the body is one and has many members, and all the members of the body, though many, are one body, so it is with Christ.   (1 Cor 12:12-13)

The "oneness" into which they are baptized, and which he preaches time and again to these various communities, moves toward the "particular." The homiletic dynamic is clear and St Paul is the example: we move from the same basic message toward the particular situation, from the universal precepts of the one Gospel, toward the given circumstance of the local community. Paul reminds each community that this oneness takes the shape of a "double heartbeat": worship (λατρεία) and service (διακονία). To effectively realize the oneness through this "double heartbeat," means that each will have to engage in a struggle against himself and his human "instincts," regardless of the particular circumstances.

> But do not live as your human flesh tells you, but live by the Spirit of God ... If you do not have the Spirit of Christ in you, you do not belong to him.
> (Rom 8:9 KJV)

Thus, their bodies are to be "dead to sin" (cf. 1 Cor 2:10-16, Rom 6:3ff) so that they may put on the "new nature" upon which their oneness in Christ can only be built:

> And put on the new nature, created after the likeness of God in true righteousness and holiness. Therefore, putting away falsehood, let every one speak the truth with his neighbor, for we are members one of another. (Eph 2:24-25)

Paul preaches that no "opportunity of the devil" (τόπον τῷ διαβόλῳ) can be allowed in the community; for the sake of oneness they must deal with their own bitterness, anger, slander, etc., and

> be kind to one another, tenderhearted, forgiving one another, as God in Christ forgave you. (Eph 4:32)

Preaching to each community the one message of the Word, e.g. oneness, St Paul is saying that in order to achieve this goal, the need is always to "close the gap" between belief and behavior. Keeping these two dynamically related, it was his "word" which actually shaped and formed each group of people as a distinct Christian community—clearly a task for the pastor who preaches today.

> ... the gap he so valiantly attempted to bridge between the ideals set forth in his Gospel and the

living-out (of those ideals) by the Christians of the
Churches he founded, of what he proudly and con-
sistently referred to as "my gospel"[12] (Rom 2:16).

In attempting to "bridge this gap," St Paul knows each
community: he is aware of where they are, what they are
doing, and how they are thinking. A further example of how
he speaks to a particular community is shown in Galatians,
as David Stanley[13] explains:

> For, to the naive Galatians, he preemptorily dismissed
> any "other gospel" as a perversion of "the gospel
> of Christ" (Gal 1:6-9), stating unequivocally that
> "the gospel proclaimed by me is no mere human in-
> vention." "Nor did I receive it from any human
> being, nor was I taught it in any other way than
> by a revelation from Jesus Christ" (Gal 1:11-12).

Paul is here warning the Galatians, over whom he
"marvels," because they have so soon forgotten the true
gospel, and instead have listened to some who pervert that
gospel. They are not to listen, "even if we, or an angel from
heaven, should preach to you a gospel contrary to that which
we preached" (cf. Gal 1:8). Paul deals with the particular
situation of the Church in Galatia.

With the Corinthians (besides the obvious moral implications—cf. 1 Cor 5), he takes issue with their particular
perversion of the gospel:

> But I am afraid ... your thoughts will be led astray
> from a sincere and pure devotion (ἁπλότητος—
> singleness) to Christ. For if some one comes and
> preaches another Jesus, ... or if you receive a dif-
> ferent spirit ... or accept a different gospel ... you
> submit to it readily enough.   (2 Cor 11:3-4 KJV)

We must restate: these examples—and there are more—

---

[12]David Stanley, "Idealism and Realism in Paul" in *The Way* [magazine]
(Middlesex, England: January 1981), p. 35.
[13]*Loc. cit.*

do not mean that St Paul ever forgets the one true message of the Word; this forms the very substance of his effort, wherever he preaches, and in whatever circumstance that his preaching shapes the community. However, the point is that Paul shows how this one true message of salvation can be applied to their predicament.

There are other examples: note his letter to Philemon, the wealthy man whose grand house was used by the Colossian community. Here Paul's "particularity" is seen as he becomes very personal with Philemon regarding the runaway Onesimos (who is not only Philemon's slave, but now his "brother" whom Paul baptized in prison). Some exegetes claim that Paul is asking for Onesimos' freedom, but whatever the purpose, the point for us is that Paul says it with these personal words:

> Yes, brother, I want some benefit from you in the Lord. Refresh my heart in Christ. Confident of your obedience, I write to you knowing that you will do even more than I say.   (Philem 1:20-21)

This is a clear example of how St Paul applies the Word to the circumstance. He is particular and personal in applying the Gospel; he does not speak in generalities in order to circumvent the particulars of those communities. He keeps together belief and behavior, worship and service, ideals and practice. In each case, the focal point of Paul's preaching is the life, death and resurrection of Christ which forms each community, not only as "one" (to use our example) but also as a "new creation" (Gal 6:15), as "reconciled" (2 Cor 2:18-19), as "free and liberated" (Gal 2:4; 5:1; Rom 6:8; 8:2), in order for them to live their lives according to such truths. St Paul is an excellent model for the contemporary pastor engaged in the ministry of the word.

5. Patristic Views of Preaching

There is continuity with St Paul's preaching in the Patristic age; the Fathers are rooted in the same Divine-human synergy, and their ministry of the word is applied to the particular circumstance of their communities. We shall deal first with St Basil and what he said *about* preaching, and then look to St John Chrysostom to see *how* he preached. This will be followed by a summary of what other Fathers said about the ministry of the Word.

St Basil is concerned about the role of the leader (*proestos*) in preaching. The first point he makes is that this leader must have a certain degree of authority when he is delivering the message (*Reg. br. 114*). He gets this authority not on his own, but precisely as a "calling" from the Holy Spirit, through the Christian community's ordination. Preaching and ordination are closely connected. One does not truly preach to those who do not recognize this authority; the choice, i.e. the *"Axios"*—the "worthy"—which is shouted out at ordination by the people is involved.

When this authority is in good order, then the leader proclaims, as St Basil says in *On Psalm 48*, as a herald (κῆρυξ), as an apostle (ἀπόστολος), and as lips of Christ (χείλη τοῦ Χριστοῦ). The priest who preaches is totally to be identified with the proclamation so that he and it become one. St Basil emphasizes this: "I bring back to you the tidings the Spirit taught me, and I say nothing of my own, nothing human" (*On Psalm 48:2*).

This identification with the proclamation has other implications for St Basil, and certainly for the contemporary preacher.

In his *Moral Rule 70*, for example, Basil says the contents of the message must be exemplified in his own life: "The leader must himself possess what he brings" and "one must not put constraint upon others to do what he has not done himself." Finally, "the leader of the word should make himself an example to others of every good thing, practic-

ing first what he teaches." In fact, in the 37th section of
Moral Rule 70, he says that the proclaimer, who is the
judging eye of the community, has to be prepared himself
to stand scrutiny and judgment "by the very people who are
entrusted to him."

In his *Epistle 150:4*, Basil says: "The instruction of how
to lead a Christian life depends less on words than on
daily living." Thus, he is not only leader of the word, but
also the servant of the word. St Gregory Nazianzen says the
same thing: How can we induce somebody to accept an
opinion which is different from that which we have taught
by our life.

On the proclamation itself, in his *Moral Rule 70*, St
Basil warns of some impediments to the preaching of the
Word:

1. The preacher must not flatter the hearers, satisfying
   their own pleasures.
2. He must not abuse his authority either to insult
   them or exalt himself over them.
3. He must not imagine that he himself is credited
   with preaching, but that he is a "co-worker" (συν-
   εργοì) with the Spirit.
4. He must not put himself at the disposal of those
   who pay special attention to him, i.e. he must not
   preach in order to receive "favors."

Finally, in his *Rule 70*, St Basil brings us very practically to the wholeness of the preacher of the Word. We
need a "boldness" (παρρησία) in proclaiming and bearing witness; we need continuous prayers for the growth of
those who receive our words; we need periodic visitations
aimed at strengthening the receivers; we need spiritual and
material assistance for the hearers who need it. We see
clearly how this is a "ministry."

Finally, St Basil says:

He who teaches should set before himself this aim:
to bring all to a perfect man, to the measure of the

stature of the fulness of Christ, yet each in his
own order.   (Rule 70:31)

St John Chrysostom, as St Basil and St Paul, applies the
Word of God to the circumstance of those to whom he is
preaching. Chrysostom uses his fine rhetorical training in
preaching the Eternal Word, proving again the effect of
the Divine-human synergy.[14]

With Chrysostom, the contemporary preacher clearly understands that there is a difference between a composition
which is read, and a sermon which is preached. In both,
human speech, effort, planning, etc. are used, but in each
they are used differently and with a different intention.

The first form that Chrysostom uses is dialogue
(*dialektikon*) and explanation (*prosopopeia*). He creates a
form of dialogue, for example, between Jesus and the un-
believing Jews at the miracle of the mulplication of the
loaves. Chrysostom would begin by saying Jesus' words:
"You follow me, not because you saw miracles, but because
you did eat of the bread and were filled." Then he would
explain: "Christ is saying here, 'You are not interested in
my miracles which attest to my divinity. You are simply
interested in eating the bread.'" Chrysostom would continue: "They do not like this rebuff and so they say, 'Our
fathers did eat manna in the desert,'" and he explains
again: "They are saying, 'The miracle which you worked
yesterday was not so great. Moses worked a greater miracle
when he fed our ancestors with manna from heaven.'" In
this manner Chrysostom would proceed to bring this miracle
to life for his community. Through the use of such dialogue
and explanation, Chrysostom would actually speak the words
of each person in the scripture, and then, be the moderator
to explain their meaning to the congregation.

Another form strings together ideas without connectives
(*asyndeton*), giving a particular force to the words; one
would hardly do this in a proper essay or composition! For

[14]This information can be found in the *Homiletic and Pastoral Review*,
February 1982. The article is entitled "A Sermon, Not an Essay" by Matthew
Reilly, who summarizes these points from a study by William Most's
entitled "A Rhetorical Study of St John Chrysostom's *De Sacerdotio*."

example, in his *On the Statues* (Hom 2): "Our calamity has become an enigma: a flight from enemies; an expulsion of inhabitants without a battle; a captivity without capture."

The use of *polysyndeton,* on the other hand, uses more connectives than necessary; this again gives a different force to the words: *On the Statues* (Hom 3):

> For as he who is humane and merciful and forgiving cuts away the greater mass of his sins, so he who is bitter and cruel and implacable, greatly increases the magnitude of his offenses.

Chrysostom also uses *rhetorical questions* which arouse the community's curiosity before he pronounces the meaning of God's Word. For example, *On the Statues* (Hom 2):

> Do you wish to be rich?
> Have God as a friend ...
> Do you wish to be rich?
> Do not be highminded.

Or in a series of questions:

> Have you a son who died prematurely?
> Say, "The Lord gives and the Lord takes away."
> Do you see your fortune exhausted?
> Say, "Naked came I out of my mother's womb."

One favorite form of Chrysostom's is the *prokataleipsis,* which anticipates objections before an opponent has a chance to raise them. Here we see how Chrysostom, as a true "pastor" who preaches, knows his parish.

> Now to prevent your saying, "How, when liable to such sins, were we justified?"

or again,

> What then, it may be said, will you say to those frequent instances of men being altered for the worse by tribulations?

The final form used by Chrysostom is that of *antithesis*. This is when the great preacher placed two ideas in opposition to each other. In this way some truth is brought out by contrast. One example refers to the ministry of the priesthood:

> It is absurd that, when they want to buy a slave they test him thoroughly, but when they elect anyone to such a ministry, they vote without inquiry.

He even applies *antithesis* to preaching itself:

> Who then, can bear the disgrace, that when he [the priest] speaks, all are still and seem bored, and look forward to the end of the discourse as to the end of suffering; while if another speaks at even greater length, they gladly pay attention, are displeased when he wishes to conclude, and are indignant when he wishes to be silent.

In these examples (of which there are many more throughout the great preacher's sermons), Chrysostom uses concrete language to present concepts—even the most lofty—from the Old and New Testament: images, comparisons, arguments, stories, examples. This, of course, should have a bearing on all those who preach today.

Many concepts gleaned from both Basil and Chrysostom's knowledge will be used later in the chapter on the contemporary challenge of preaching. But first we will briefly see what some other Fathers say regarding this ministry.

Other Fathers

Besides St Basil and St John Chrysostom, there are others who spoke directly about the homiletic task. We shall end this first section on the early roots of preaching by letting these Fathers "speak for themselves."

St **Gregory the Great** understood the relationship between study and preaching, saying that one must never stop reading:

> Now, all this is duly fulfilled by the pastor if, being inspired by the supernal spirit of fear and love, he meditates diligently and every day on the precepts of the sacred word. The words of divine admonition should restore in him the sense of responsibility, which habitual intercourse with men constantly destroys. One who protracts length of years in secular society should . . . (be in the) pursuit of instruction. It is evidently necessary that they who devote them selves to the office of preaching should never depart from the occupation of sacred reading . . . Let the teachers, ever meditating in their hearts on the sacred word . . . teach forthwith when the occasion demands it. (*Pastoral Care* 2:11, p. 86ff, *ACW*)

St **Ambrose of Milan** held that teaching is a necessity in the life of the priest. Ambrose claims that this position, listed last by St Paul is for him first, since by it he is always learning.

> We can no longer flee from the duty of teaching, which the necessity of priestly life imposes on our reluctant shoulders. For "his gifts were that some should be apostles, some prophets, some evangelists, some pastors and teachers" (Eph 4:11). I do not claim the glory of the apostles for myself. Who can do this, if not chosen by the Son of God? I do not long to attain the grace of the prophets, nor the power of the evangelists, nor the circumspection of pastors; I am striving only after that understanding and diligence in regard to the sacred scriptures which the Apostle lists as the last of the duties of the saints. My reason for this is that by teaching I learn. For there is only one true master who did not learn those things which he taught to all.
> (*On the Duties of the Ministers* 1, bff, *P.L.,* 16:27.)

St Augustine in a letter written to Bishop Valerius shortly after his ordination to the priesthood, knew that the preacher needs to study, and thus begged the bishop for the time to prepare himself. Valerius (whose Latin was very poor!) commissioned the young priest to preach in the cathedral, a great honor which was rarely given. This task was so great that Augustine felt "tormented," "weighed down," and "not fit" for the task.

> If the Lord did this, not as a punishment, but out of mercy . . . I ought to study all his remedies in the scriptures, and, by praying and reading so to act that strength sufficient for such perilous duties may be granted to my soul. I did not do this before, because I did not have time, but as soon as I was ordained, I planned to use all my leisure time in studying the sacred scriptures, and I tried to arrange to have leisure for this task. Truly, I did not know what I needed for such a task, but now I am tormented and weighed down by it. If I have learned by experience what is needful for a man who administers the sacrament and the word of God to the people—and I do not lay claim to what I do not possess—do you, Father Valerius, give me a command which is my destruction? Where is your charity? Do you truly love me? Do you truly love the Church itself, to which you wish me to minister? I am sure you love both me and the Church, but you consider me fit, whereas I know myself better. And I should not have known myself if I had not learned by experience.
>
> (*Letter* 21:3-6, *FC* pp. 40-51)

St Gregory Nazianzen, always concerned with dogma, ends his *Second Oration* with a call for the proper dispensation of the word. It is only in listening to the Spirit that one may "regulate with judgment the truth of our dogmas." In fact, Gregory claims it is not within the power of "every man's intellect" to expound this dogma, and that even for those who do have this power, the "aid of the Spirit is required":

We come now to the dispensation of the word, so that in conclusion we may speak of what comes first in our ministry. Everyone is ready to discourse upon that divine and exalted word, but I am amazed at the intelligence, not to say the folly, of anyone who boldly undertakes it and supposes that it is within the power of every man's intellect. To me indeed it seems no slight task, and one requiring no little spiritual power, to give in due season to each his portion of the word, and to regulate with judgment the truth of our dogmas ... Now this involves a very great risk to those who are charged with the illumination of others, if they are to avoid (error) ... A suitable and worthy comprehension and exposition of this subject demand a discussion of greater length than the present occasion, or even our life, allows. Most especially, now and at all times, the aid of the Spirit is required by whom alone we are able to perceive, to expound, or to embrace the truth in regard to God.

(NPNF, p. 212 ff.)

St Gregory the Great of Rome adds these thoughts on the teaching of dogma in this ministry:

No one ventures to teach any art unless he has learned it after deep thought. With what rashness, then, would the pastoral office be undertaken by the unfit, seeing that the government of souls is the art of arts. For who does not realize that the wounds of the mind are more hidden than the internal wounds of the body? Yet ... people who are utterly ignorant of spiritual precepts, are often not afraid of professing themselves to the physicians of the heart ... They crave to appear as teachers and covet ascendancy over others, and, as the Truth attests: "They seek the first salutations in the market place, the first places at feasts, and the first chairs in the synagogues."

(*Pastoral Care,* Mt 23:6ff *ACW* 1, 1, p. 21)

Then the great pope links his concern with the entire range of pastoral care in which the pastor preaches for the wrong reasons (conceit, vanity, cupidity, etc.).

These persons are all the more unfitted to administer worthily what they have undertaken, the office of pastoral care, in that they have attained to the tutorship of humility by vanity alone: for, obviously, in this tutorship the tongue purveys mere jargon when one thing is learned and its contrary taught... These reign by their own conceit, not the will of the Supreme Ruler; they are sustained by no virtues, are not divinely called, but being inflamed by their cupidity, they seize, rather than attain supreme rule.
                    (*Pastoral Care, ACW* 11, 21 f.)

But finally it is Chrysostom who summarizes this concern for preaching by referring to the "spoken word" as the "sole instrument," the only "method of cure," which stands against "false doctrine."

In the spiritual order, however, it is useless to consider physical remedies. Save for good example, there is but one means and method of cure; the spoken word. This is the sole instrument, the only diet, the finest climate. It takes the place of medication, of cautery, and the knife... When it is a question of the soul being sickened by false doctrine, then there is a great need for preaching, not only to maintain safety at home, but also to war against the enemy outside. If a man possessed the sword of the spirit and the shield of faith to such an extent that he could work miracles... he would have little need of preaching. No, I say, even then it would not be useless, but quite necessary. The blessed Paul made use of preaching, although he was renowned everywhere on account of his miracles... It was only so that they might have leisure for the ministry of the word that all the apostles in one accord entrusted the care of the widows to Stephen.   (*On the Priesthood,* Bk 4:3-5)

Chrysostom is the one who leads us from these early roots of preaching into the contemporary challenge of the ministry of the word. We must allow his words to guide us in this task, for he knows that the priest who preaches, must both "arm himself with the power of the word," and must use "great prudence" to lead the community away from "idle speculation." In all this, Chrysostom says, "he has no other assistance than the preaching of the word."

We must strive diligently to obtain the power of eloquence, unless we already possess the power of miracles. Since, however, not a vestige of this latter power remains with us, and our enemies continue to attack us on every side, we must arm ourselves with the power of the word, lest we be struck by the darts of the enemy, and so that we may strike them in turn .... when a man uses his authority to stop the mouths of the curious, he merely earns the reputation of being proud and ignorant. For this reason the superior [priest] requires great prudence so that in leading his people away from such idle speculations, he can keep himself clear of the above-mentioned charges. In all this he has no assistance other than the preaching of the word; and if he have no talent for this, then the souls of those men in his charge will fare no better than ships tossed in the storm. I speak, of course, of those who are the weaker and more curious among them. It behooves a priest, therefore, to do everything possible to obtain this proficiency!   (*On the Priesthood,* 4:3-5)

CHAPTER SIX

Contemporary Preaching

In the previous chapter, we concluded with a call from Chrysostom for "proficiency," and having previously taken into account the early roots of preaching, we can now ask what this means for the proclamation in our contemporary situation.

There are three concerns in this chapter: (1) The Word and "words": what to preach, (2) The form of preaching in the liturgical cycle and (3) preaching the "story" (*mythos*) of Christian peoplehood.

1. The Word and "words"

In a sense the question of "what is preached" has already been answered: "Jesus is the Lord." This essential, "always-the-same" message, and all that goes with it, forms the substance of all Christian preaching. What, however, constitutes the specific contents of our preaching; what are the *changeable* elements within this *unchangeable* message?

It must first be said that in order to preach, one must know the Gospel, not merely something *about* it, but truly *know* it. Secondly—and here is where the concern for "ministry" enters—the proclamation of the Word can never be separated from how the community is *cared* for. This is most obvious in the previous section on Patristic preaching: the ministry of the Word is a central part of a proper pastoral care or pastoral ministry.

155

This is further revealed when placed in the context of a present day parish: if a person of faith (the condition changes if the hearer does not have faith) hears a sermon and goes away from the liturgy asking the question, "But what does that sermon have to do with my life as a Christian being?" do we not have to wonder whether or not the Gospel has been properly proclaimed, or if that person has been properly cared for? There may be a deficiency here in the ministry of the Word.

The connection is obvious in this case: preaching is part of pastoral care because it is a word spoken verbally and powerfully by the preacher (who in most cases *is* the pastor), in order to change or influence those who hear those words. The principle of caring as a pastor is precisely the same, even if the form may be different.

The intent is that

> preaching changes people, or at least "good preaching" does. Such preaching is said to combine a strong biblical thrust with good illustrative material and personal charism, and be capable of influencing persons at their deepest levels of meaning and motivation, if not indeed "changing their lives."[1]

In fact, Arthur Teikmanis in *Preaching and Pastoral Care* simply says: "dynamic preaching is basically pastoral care in the context of worship."[2]

If this is true, we can then ask: "What is needed to change—to convert—people through preaching? How is it, in fact and indeed, a 'ministry'?"

To answer this question means first to deal with the dynamic meaning of "words" as a reflection of *The Word*.

> The Word is not merely the Book or even a message which the Book tells about, and a word is not merely a sound or a particular patterning of ink on a page.

[1]Rodney Hunter, "Ministry or Magic?" *Chandler Review*, May 1976, p. 13.
[2]Arthur Teikmanis, *Preaching and Pastoral Care* (Englewood, N.J., 1964) p. 19.

The word "word" refers to the self-expression of a person. It is initiative-taking in the communication of oneself. It is the personal act of self-revelation. It is the making exterior of that which is interior to one's own being, whether spoken by God or by a human being.[3]

If it is a "communication of oneself," "self-expression," "initiative-taking," etc., then obviously the truth is that a word is never *merely* a word. It is a relation and manifestation of both, the being who speaks it, and of his intent in its "spokenness." When that "Being" is God, the implications, which we learn from the Genesis account of creation (and later from the Prologue of St John), are obvious. And here it must be said that although our focus is on the "ministry," and not centered on the "dogma" ("theology") of the Word as such, this "theological" meaning must first be clarified and established: "Any analysis of the biblical material shows the identification of the Word of God with the act of God."[4] This is why Christ, as the Second Person of the Trinity, is called *The Word*. In other words, the scripture tells us clearly that the Word has the power to create, to produce order within creation, and to restore; when God the Word speaks (as at creation and in the incarnation) things change, people change, something is done.

This also has meaning for "words" which are spoken by the preacher, because we learn that when they are spoken, an "event" happens; this, after all, is no mere transmission of facts and information. Rather, the "strange thing" that happens, to which we pointed earlier, occurs in order for that pastor who preaches, to "touch and stretch" the people whom he leads, i.e. to *change* them.

When God speaks, he acts to establish, sustain, and build communion with us. When we as preachers preach the Word, that is, speak words in a certain

[3]David Switzer, *Pastor, Preacher, Person* (Nashville Tenn.: Abingdon, 1979) p. 55.
[4]*Ibid.,* p. 57.

way in a specific context, God speaks his Word to elicit our response in relation to him.[5]

This connection between the Word and "words" is even extended: when one preaches the Word through his many and various human words, those words are always tested and validated by their congruence with *The Word.*

Only those human words which can stand the scrutiny of this Word (Christ), which indeed convey him in some sense by means of their human speaking, can appropriately be called the Word of God.[6]

The words which we speak, then, convey the truth about Christ the Word, and are thus responses to his ministry in which we serve; they are responses which seek to change persons according to the purposes realized in his "self-oblation." When God speaks, he acts to establish and build communion with others. The human words which must transmit and be congruent with the Word, are then words of *communion* (which is no mere mechanical process) in which the inner being of a person is communicated to others. The words which are spoken are to facilitate, to prepare the soil of the soul, to cause the heart to be receptive and responsive to the Word of God, as it now flows through our human words. Surely this is a central function of pastoral care; preaching, in this case, falls fully within the scope of "ministering" on the part of the pastor.

Thus the words which are spoken are, in the deepest sense, words which express how persons are cared for—a true definition of Christian pastoral care through the ministry of the Word. "What" is preached, therefore, interacts with all that is attempted in the pastor's ministry.

Although this is not a liturgical study, it should be said here that, for the priest, this is also true in terms of worship in the liturgical life. Homiletics may indeed be studied by itself, just as hymnology may be studied by itself, but these

[5]*Ibid.,* p. 60.
[6]*Ibid.,* p. 61.

are only *realized* as liturgy. This is true because the liturgy seeks to bring God and man into communion; preaching enunciates the faith upon which that communion is realized.

2. A Preaching Model in the Liturgical Cycle

As is well known to any person who has preached, this is more difficult than it sounds. Suddenly it becomes a question of how this great challenge can be realized, that is, "how can I preach The Word through the 'words'?"

Without submitting totally to "techniques," we can point to a general model which, though not prescriptive, combines the wisdom and practice of earlier preachers with what seems necessary for our contemporary Christian communities.

First, the minds of those present must be penetrated—even "shakened." Chrysostom did this very well. This is necessary, for the hearers may not *want* to hear anything challenging, upsetting or revealing, in terms of their most "comfortable" life. (In fact some persons would prefer to remain in misery than to change!) They may be thinking about who is coming to dinner, or what happened at work last Friday, or what the doctor's report will say, etc. But whatever it is, the attention of the parish can never be assumed; it must be "crashed-through." This is especially true today, given the type of "immediate" communication-entertainment world in which we live. Their attention needs first to be aroused, then captured and held! They must know that this preacher (pastor) truly *cares* for them, for their life and faith, that he cares what comes from his mouth in attempting to lead them to this "change." Remembering what Chrysostom says, this "rational flock" must be respected in one's preaching, not constantly berated and scolded. Thus, if there are "cobwebs" present, if the attitude is one of "ho-hum" to begin with, the first few statements of the introduction must "crash through" all that is presently occupying the attention of the hearers.

As a preacher, the minister of the Word must ask, "how can I use myself—as an instrument—to enable the

Holy Spirit to enter their minds and hearts?" Questions—the interrogative—and stories are excellent ways to begin. Both have been used time and again in the past. The preacher must win the attention of his listeners in the very first minute, must already respond to a hypothetical question on the parish's part: "Why should I listen to his words?" Or again, "Is he proclaiming the Word with some investment of his own self?" or even again, "Is his faith contagious? Does he believe what he is saying?" A lethargic instrument (preacher) will probably instill a lethargic response.

Secondly, the preacher must offer concrete examples. This is the area where images, ideas, illustrations, etc., must be given in order to support what is ideally, *one single objective* (given also in the introduction) of the preacher's sermon. This is also done throughout the Old and New Testament, for example, in the prophets and in the parables and metaphors of Christ. Here the real substance—the "body" of the sermon—must be transmitted.

Finally, the conclusion—the "so what" or the "therefore"—must be given. Here is the "thus saith the Lord" which is the preacher's final point. Actually, from the beginning, the hearers have already been asking themselves: "so what?" That is, "he has aroused our sleeping souls and hearts, he has developed his point, but now we want to know what this *means,* or how this is to *be applied.*" In other words, there is here a resolution of expectancy which has been raised in their minds, and this must be concretized in the ending.

This is a very general model in a simplified form, but in fact, it should be, in order to make its point: preaching should never be academic, it should vary from person to person, and should always leave room for God to work.

It must also be said, in terms of "what to preach," that the Church's *lectionary* of epistles and gospels does not limit the scope of the proclamation. In fact, just the opposite is true, if the preacher is truly in touch with the meaning of the liturgical cycle (in its various forms), and if he remembers that it contains all that is truly essential for living the Christian life. Of course, his own energy, his own interest, his own prayer life, will always be involved in what he makes of it for his parish. Thus, although the central idea may be given through a theme or a text in the cycle, the controlling objective and orientation of this "given" is clearly part of the effort of the preacher.

For example, within this liturgical rhythm, the believing community can be led by the preacher to understand the deepest and most objective messages of the Gospel in terms of their own lives (thus enabling this community to make deeper changes because of the message). Some examples are the following: *Advent*: waiting, expectation, promise; *Christmas*: Christ's birth and incarnation in our lives, stirrings, growing spiritually; *Epiphany*: how God reveals himself to us, light, manifestation, its connection with the Nativity; *Triodion and Great Lent*: Christ's sacrifice and the place of sacrificial love and repentance in our lives; *Easter*: Resurrection and death in our own lives, hope, forgiveness; *Pentecost*: life, spirit, renewal, recreation; *Trinity*: community of faith, community of persons, etc.; *Hagiography*: Saints' lives and our own, etc.

These are only some themes within these given cycles. But throughout, the aim is to lead persons to know that God is near, and that the great themes, the stories and the examples, which are there to constantly remind them of this truth, have implications for their own Christian living!

Study and preparation by the preacher is crucial, even given the themes of the cycles; the pattern does not preclude the "struggle" in preaching. Any good concordance can help prepare the preaching for this liturgical cycle. For example, themes appear again and again (and can be found in any concordance) in the Old and New Testaments: give/take/receive; work/rest; die/born again; burdens imposed/burdens lifted; sin/repentance/forgiveness; hunger/eat/thirst/drink; waiting/fulfillment; sickness/healing; fear/peace; dark/light; slavery/liberation. And so on. These speak to the person's own spiritual response to the "wonderful work of God."

It must also be said that the preacher should not only identify with Christ, but also with the message; *we* (in-

cluding the preacher) are the hungry man, the blind, the
lame, the prodigal, the Samaritan woman; *we* are the one
in whom "demons lurk"; *we* are those who come to Christ
to be fed and forgiven, or for hope when our son or
daughter is dead. Again, these are all in the specific "whats"
in preaching, the "words" of the Word.

Finally, in terms of "what to preach," the forms themselves need not be closed because of the liturgical cycle.
Hermeneutics, which refers to the interpretation of God's
word, is best realized in those forms in which persons can
truly grasp the transmission of thought. James Cox, in
Biblical Preaching, points to some of these "forms" which
are in continuity with the liturgical cycle. The first form is
the *classic homily*—"the verse-by-verse, phrase-by-phrase . . .
treatment of a text . . . (which is) at one and the same time
the easiest and the hardest."[7] He places this "form," which
we have seen Chrysostom and the other Fathers use, in
these terms:

> If you think it is easy, you will be superficial, repetitive
> and boring; if you come to the challenge of a passage
> such as Jacob meeting the angel at Jabbok, you will
> wrestle with it and not let go until the text blesses
> both you and those who are under your spiritual care.[8]

A second "form," continuous with the cycle, is the power
of a *story.* This has already been mentioned in terms of
describing a story within the Scripture, e.g. the healing of
the paralytic or the multiplication of loaves. If the scene is
made alive for the parishioners, they will see themselves
as both the paralytic, and as those who "help" him (by
lowering him through the roof), or even, as those who
"pressed up" to the Lord in that hot and dusty Palestinian
house, in order to hear his words. Other stories are also
valuable: the Desert Fathers, the lives of Saints, etc. do
not conflict with the liturgical cycle, and can be used to
support the given theme.

[7]James Cox, *A Guide to Biblical Preaching* (Nashville, Tenn.: Abingdon,
1976) p. 22.
[8]*Ibid.,* p. 23.

The use of *multiple* texts is a third form which can be used with the liturgical cycle, but this requires more work on the part of the preacher. The Patristic preachers often did this. For example, the ancient question in the Book of Job, "If a man die, shall he live again," can easily be compared with the words of Christ in St John: "He that lives and believes in me shall never die" (John 11:26). Another example is when God asks Adam: "Where art thou?" (Gen 3:9) or the text in St Matthew's Gospel: "Where is he that is born king of the Jews?" (Mt 2:2), which can be compared with and answered by, "I came to seek and save that which was lost" (Lk 9:10). These, of course, are only two examples; the possibilities are endless.

But whatever the form, which need not be limited by the content of the given liturgical cycle of the Church, the preacher should explain what needs explaining, and no more than that! Here it is always good to remember:

Recognize your human inability to explain some things. The Bible itself is full of God, but nowhere does it undertake a systematic explanation of him. When the apostle Paul takes on the task of justifying the ways of God to man, he breaks off, exclaiming: "O depth of wealth, wisdom and knowledge in God! How unsearchable his judgments, how untraceable His ways" (Rom 11:33).[9]

3. Preaching the Story of Peoplehood

Finally, what must be said in this particular section on contemporary preaching has to do with preaching the "story" of the Christian people. We must understand why this concept of "story" is so crucial to the ministry of the Word. First we must see the story in relationship to peoplehood, then see how it functions in biblical history.

What seems to be missing in our contemporary proclamation is not that we do not know what has happened; God

[9]*Ibid.,* p. 35.

has revealed himself, i.e. he has created us, saved us, and continues in his saving work. Rather, what is missing today is that we seem to have forgotten that we are telling this story! In fact, we Christians have forgotten that we are a people with a story, we are an "inheritance." We need only to recall the hymn sung in the Orthodox Church on the Feast of the Cross: "O, Lord save thy people and bless thine inheritance." If we are a people and an inheritance, there is a story which explains that inheritance, or rather, a story about what it is which we have indeed inherited. Wherever there is a "people," there is a story which holds them together, cements them, binds them. They are a part of this story. They remember this story. They continue to tell this story. They have a fidelity to this story.

We are here to tell the story of God and his people (or to say it in another way, to tell the story of our Christian peoplehood). Here we come to the valuable meaning of the term "mythos." By this word "mythos," we do not mean a "false story": the use of the word with this meaning we are warned about in Scripture, i.e. not to believe in "myths" and in "fables" (e.g. 2 Tim 4:4). This understanding has come down to us in our secular language as something like: "Oh that's not true, that's a myth." This meaning of a false story, however, is not what the biblical exegetes or religious anthropologists mean by this word in its relationship to peoplehood.

More positively, the word "mythos," in its proper spiritual context, means an *inner and collective experience* of the people, carried precisely in a shared story (in fact, in generations of experience which are shared). The story *carries* the mythos, carries the sacred experience. We define and measure that experience today against those generations that have experienced it before us—and have told the story!

This story is what we live by; our values and attitudes are shaped by it; this is the faith that is carried from father to son, through the generations. This makes it not a "false story," but an organic and special story. For example, we tell the story of Adam and Eve and how "they took the apple." The mythos of the story is not about the apple, but carries the truth that "pride goes before the fall." That experience, transmitted in the story, is eternally true!

This is the most positive and beneficial meaning of this term "mythos," which is transmitted in order to define our Christian peoplehood: it is not a kind of "cerebral" or intellectual thesis; it is rooted in the Christian soul—it penetrates and binds the community. It is out of this community which shares the story that true Christian personhood is born. The community carries this inner story which tells us who we are; it tells us what we are to be; it tells us how we are to take our journey through life; it tells us in what to have hope and faith; it tells us who we are as creature and who God is as Creator; it tells us, as all the generations before us knew and lived by, what are our limits and what are our possibilities before the face of God. For Christians, it tells us that only God is our refuge; as the Orthodox sing in their doxology, "Thou art our refuge in all generations." Our "mythos," then, is the story of our inner experience and vision as a Christian people. Thus, it explains what we must proclaim in the ministry of the Word.

Story in the Old and New Israel

Our point about this organic and special story can be seen in this word μῦθος in its original Greek.[10]

In examining the word, one finds that it means "anything delivered by word of mouth": it is a "word," it is "speech," it is "conversation," it is "the subject, the thing, the matter itself"; it is a "saying," it is "what was seen," it is a "proverb." *Mythologos* is a "teller of the word." And this word, as we have seen, gives shape and meaning; it forms and creates.

This is clearly seen in biblical history. The Israelites become a "people" when they are led out of Egypt in the Exodus: *then* they tell the stories, then they proclaim the

[10]Here I used Liddell and Scott's *Greek-English Lexicon* (7th Edition) Oxford: Clarendon Press, 1872 from which all the following definitions of μῦθος are taken.

"mythos" which explains their peoplehood and which binds them as a people (and then, for example, they tell what happens in Genesis).[11]

Looking already at the Israel of the Old Testament in terms of what the "story" meant to them, it seems true to say, then, that one of the contemporary problems faced by any person who preaches in the ministry of the Word, is simply that the people have forgotten their story. A further truth can immediately be stated: if the people do not have this "mythos," there will always be *some* story which is seeking to form them—and herein lies the "false story," the negative use of the myth, which will be oriented toward the secular, career, possession, etc., which seeks to influence their identity as a "people."

Looking into the New Testament, we find the same thing. Although not the exclusive factor, when our Lord wants to "form his people" (the new Israel, the new creation), he tells the story of the Good Samaritan (and it is clearly not a true story, as such) which is told in response to the lawyer's question of "inheriting eternal life" (Lk 10:30-37). Here he speaks a narrative: parable (παραβολή) means, in the literal sense, the "conveying of the lesson." While it is true that many of our Lord's parables, especially those referring to the Kingdom of Heaven, were intended for various reasons to convey an obscure and enigmatic lesson, the point (the truth) of being a good neighbor is quite clearly carried by this parable—by this mythos-story.[12] In fact, Christ does not even say who is the good neighbor. Instead, this mythos-story, in order to stimulate a response, ends with the interrogative: "Now

[11]I owe this explanation to Rev. Dr. Paul Tarazi, Professor of Old Testament at St Vladimir's Orthodox Seminary, Crestwood, N.Y., who made this point at a Clergy Symposium in Chicago, July 1980.
[12]When I first developed this point of the parabolic story, I used much of Joachim Jeremias' material, but I used especially Jules Lebreton, S.J. *The Life and Teaching of Jesus Christ* (London: Burns and Oats, 1957), Chapter VII, "The Parables of the Kingdom." There it explains in detail the use and method of the parables of the Kingdom in its fullest extent. However, my initial intent was simply to show the relationship of the parabolic story to the formation of the Christian peoplehood, and not a study, as such, of the parable. Since that time, however, I was reminded that it might be wise to include this more exacting nature of the parable, lest it appear more

who do *you* think is the good neighbor?" It carries the
obvious conclusion within it: "Go and do likewise" (vs.

simplistic than it truly is. For this purpose I returned to Lebreton who
makes the following points:

(1) He begins that chapter (VII) by reminding the reader that "instruction by means of parables was a new method in Our Lord's ministry"
(p. 243)

(2) that regarding the parables of the Kingdom, the disciples alone,
and not those outside, were ultimately given the solutions to those parables
which were told with some obscurity (p. 243)

(3) that "the parables are not without obscurity expressly intended to
punish the Jews for their *blindness to the truth*" (p. 246)

(4) that "by the slightly enigmatic form of his parables, Jesus wished
to *provoke inquiries* and *stimulate interest*" (p. 247)

(5) that Jesus "could only impart knowledge as *they were able to
bear it,* and this resulted in some obscurity, or at least incompleteness, in
the parables which were the vehicles of his teachings" (p. 248)

(6) that, actually and paradoxically, "that for the disciples . . . it was
the obscurity of the parables by which they were *taught*" (p. 249)

(7) that it was the peoples' own *blindness* which compelled Jesus to
often teach in "veiled" parables, although "a *transparent* veil, no doubt for
those who had the will and knowledge to look beneath it" (p. 253)

However, regarding my own point in terms of the story in its relationship to "peoplehood," Lebreton says it this way: "The teaching of the
parables would show them how everything around them in daily life could
be used to express the mysteries of the Kingdom" (p. 266)

Emphasizing this very point of the transparent aspect of the parable,
which was my original point in the text, i.e.—regarding the story and
peoplehood, St John Chrysostom (P.G. LVIII, p. 473) says:

Do not say that he spoke obscurely; people could come to him and
ask him questions, as the disciples did; but they would not because
they were idle and given over to the things of self. Why do I say,
"they would not?" Because they did the exact opposite, for not only
did they not believe, not only did they not listen, but they attacked
him, and took ill what they heard him say . . .

Then Chrysostom adds:

If he did not wish the Jews to be saved, he needed only to be
silent; there was no need for him to speak in parables; but he wanted
to stimulate them by the very obscurity of his words.

In the end, the three we have chosen (The Good Samaritan, the Story
of the Barns, and The Prodigal Son) seem to be not of the obscure type,
but rather, regarding those certain lessons of the Christian life, seem to be
quite apparent. If there is anything more exegetically precise than this in
these parables, the exposure of such facts was not my original purpose. Of
the various types of parables, then (for example: those veiled in obscurity
about which the disciples ask, those which Our Lord seems immediately to
explain, and those which seem to be apparent) we point only to those
apparent parables in relationship to the formation of the Christian peoplehood.

37). To be part of this Christian people means to "look
with compassion, and cross over the road." The story which
carries the message is the Parable of the Good Samaritan.

Another example can be used, and again, not with-
standing the possibility of obscurity in such parables, we
can see a relationship of story to peoplehood. If to be a
person in this inheritance, means to seek *first* the Kingdom
of God, Jesus tells a story about "barns" (Lk 12:16-31)
and the story's import for peoplehood is what will happen
to us and to those barns if we "lay up treasures on the
earth; moth and rust will corrupt them"(Mt 6:19).

And still another. If to be a person in this inheritance,
means that when we "fall" we are to return in repentance
(and that God will be there to accept us), then Jesus tells
a story about the Prodigal Son (Lk 15:11-32). This "story of
return and reconciliation" is truly the experience of the
people of God from the beginning of time. Here we even
find a direct analogy of various stories within the same
"mythos," i.e. when we compare the story of the prodigal
son with the story of Israel: they, time and again, will also
waste what they have on "riotous living" and will have to
return to the Father who is always waiting. (In fact, they
are here often referred to in the singular, "my *son* Israel.")
In this common "mythos" we see that God continues to
abide, to wait, for them (Israel) and for him (the Prodigal).
He cannot bear to see them lost. He looks for their return.

Finally, of course, it is necessary to tell the story of
Jesus himself—a story from creation to redemption which
St Stephen the Martyr told. It is by way of remembering the
actual facts of this story that the "mythos"—the true inner
and collective experience of Christian people—is preserved.
In this way, precisely by preaching this story, we remember
who we are, as we are told who we are. This "story" then,
which is not a myth, not a fable, not a false story, is one
that carries the "mythos," the inner truth through which
we participate in the Kingdom. It is finally transmitted in
our Lord's words: "Do this in remembrance of me . . . as
often as you eat . . . as often as you drink" (1 Cor 11:23-26).

The remembrance of Jesus, the eating and the drinking:

this is who we are as a people and an inheritance. This must be the organic and special story which we proclaim in the contemporary ministry of the Word.

4. The "ministry" of the Ministry of the Word

We began this section on the ministry of the Word with the truth that a "strange thing" happens when the Word is proclaimed. We have tried to support this through an overview of the early roots of preaching, and also within the realms of contemporary preaching. In both cases, we saw that the Divine-human dynamic (synergy) best defines that "strange thing." Within that Divine-human dynamic, we recall God's Word (to Moses): "My presence will go with you," and the human word (Moses to God): "If thy presence will not go with me, do not carry us up from this place" (Ex 33:14-15). It is from this point that the preacher begins: with a "response" rather than an initiative.

In the Old and New Testament, in the Patristic era, and up to the contemporary age, preaching the Word of God, with all the human input possible, was always a *response*.

If one were to graphically attempt to describe the process which is truly inclusive of both the ministry of the clergy and of the laity, i.e. the process in which the human responds to God's initiative in his own "ministry," it would look like the following.

Divine-Human Dynamic in Homiletics

Source (God)	Transmitter (Human)	Hermeneutic (Preaching)	Learned (Hearer)	Lived (Belief and act)
|	|	|	|	
Link 1 (Theology)	Link 2 (Interpretation)	Link 3 (Translation)	Link 4 (Application)	

This model is quite obvious. God as the Source begins by creating and saving the world through communion. This truth is received by the one who is to transmit it (*Trans-*

mitter) to others (e.g. Ezekiel "eats the scroll"). It must then be preached to others in an understandable way (*Hermeneutic*), through the ministry of the clergy. Philip asked him, "Do you understand what you are reading?" "How can I understand," the Ethiopian replied, "unless someone explains it to me?" (Acts 8:30-31). It is received by the hearer (*Learned*) who is to believe and act (*Lived*) in the ministry of the laity. This is, of course, ideal and somewhat simplistic, but it does serve as a basis upon which to build a homiletic model.

The "links" by which this happens are also obvious. *Theology* is what must be first understood (Link 1), as that which is preserved and taught by the Church. The preacher must interpret that theology in his own mind, with "struggle" (Link 2). Then he must translate what he comes to understand to the parish (Link 3). Finally, this must be followed up by seeing it applied (Link 4) in the life of the people. It must be made perfectly clear, that the ministry of the Word, precisely as "ministry," is not completed until it reaches this very last stage where it is applied in the parish and where the people in their own "ministry" are led to believe and act. Other programs, educational and otherwise, are obviously part of this follow-up. In fact the "ministry" of the Word is nothing less than this entire process, from the Source to the application, in which the full range of the Ministry of the Church is evident.

PART III

THE MINISTRY OF SPIRITUAL COUNSEL

"And all this is from God, who through Christ reconciled us to himself and gave us the ministry of reconciliation."

(2 Corinthians 5:18)

CHAPTER SEVEN

Growth Into True Life

A brother questioned an old man, saying, "Here are two brothers. One of them leads a solitary life for six days a week, giving himself much pain, and the other serves the sick. Whose work does God accept with the greater favour?" The old man said, "Even if the one who withdraws for six days were to hang himself up by his nostrils, he could not equal the one who serves the sick."[1]

This story from the *The Sayings of the Desert Fathers* (*Apophthegmata Patrum*) leads us well into this chapter. It does so not because the solitary life is wrong (in fact it is most valuable and needed in the Christian life), but only because of our orientation. The emphasis is on *diakonia*—active service—in this aspect of ministry.

1. The True Aim of Personal Direction

The "ministry" of spiritual counsel—sometimes called spiritual direction—is not (as in the secular sense) "therapeutic," although it is true that in theological terms, the ministry leads to the only true therapy.[2] What is meant by

---

[1]Benedicta Ward, SLG trans. *The Wisdom of the Desert Fathers* (Fairacres, England: SLG Press, 1977) p. 61.

[2]Cf. "The Being in Act of Theology" in *Orthodox Synthesis* (Crestwood, NY: St Vladimir's Press, 1981) p. 105 in which this term is explained as θεραπεία Θεοῦ and having truly and originally been the task of the Church rather than the secular psychology.

173

174 THE MINISTRY OF THE CHURCH

this *true* therapy is that the inner healing or wholeness of a person ultimately has to do with a healing relationship with God; these two are inextricably bound to each other. The ascetic fathers always knew that the inner wholeness of the person was the true gateway to a wholeness with God. What this means is that one does not approach God without first dealing with his own life, whether within himself (mind and heart, body and spirit) or between himself and his "brother." In the secular sense, this intimate connection, this "whole picture," has been lost, thus changing the ultimate meaning of "therapy"; in the secular world one need not be concerned at all about God. In terms of ministry, however, it is precisely this "whole picture" which must be understood and maintained.

In his book *Soul Friend,* Kenneth Leech reviews the current pastoral counselling movement and seeks to clarify the difference between some of the contemporary practices of pastoral counselling and the specific Christian tradition of spiritual counsel and direction. In the chapter entitled "Directions, Counselling and Therapy," he makes four points, each having an important bearing on our particular task.

The first difference is that "the pastoral counselor's concern has tended to be with states of emotional distress."[3] Leech points to the current concern with problems and problem-solving, emotional strain and periods of crisis. He is quick, however, to say:

> Of course, there are parallels with the spiritual director, who is also involved with the experience of distress and with periods of crisis. But, pastoral care in the Christian understanding is not restricted to the troubled or distressed or to crisis points in life.[4]

The second difference is that the current practice seems to be "clinic-based or office-based rather than church-based or community-based."[5]

[3]Kenneth Leech, *Soul Friend* (San Francisco, CA, Harper & Row Publishers, 1977) p. 100.
[4]*Ibid.,* Leech.
[5]*Ibid.,* p. 101.

Thirdly, "the movement has tended to focus excessively on the problems of individuals"[6] at the expense of what he refers to as a proper social concern.

Fourthly (although Leech groups this point with the previous one) "adjustment to society ... and a freedom from anguish and attainment of peace"[7] seems to be the goal of some current counselling practices.

Leech also deals with many other factors such as "spiritual direction and the unconscious," sexuality, aberrations of religion, etc., but as important as these are, they are not immediately relevant to our point.

In each case, Leech issues a warning through these distinctions. He knows, however, that although pastoral care should never be so restricted, the pastor or Christian counselor in some way will have to come to terms with each of these specific concerns as he ministers to persons. To show what he calls an "overlap," for example, Leech makes these points: "The priest, by virtue of his cure of souls, is plunged into the area of the psyche,"[8] and later, "The aim of spiritual direction is the achievement of wholeness in life, an integrated personality, in which inner and outer man are united."[9] He says finally:

> The priest is primarily concerned with spirituality as the fundamental requirement of health. The therapist or counselor is primarily concerned with sickness. They move within the same realm of reality, so it is not surprising that there is considerable overlap.[10]

Leech's warnings are good and for this reason his book should be read by every pastoral counselor today. These warnings tell those in the ministry of spiritual counsel that the scope of their concern is beyond individual "problem solving" in any of these various forms (and each of his four points can be subsumed under this particular issue).

[6]*Ibid.*, 102.
[7]*Loc. cit.*
[8]*Ibid.*, p. 105.
[9]*Ibid.*, p. 109.
[10]*Ibid.*, p. 110.

His warning, then, is a defense against this type of "reductionism" in the pastoral ministry, where the "whole picture" is indeed lost.

If Leech's warning is in this direction, Alexander Schmemann's warning is in the other direction: the non-application of theology. In *Church, World, Mission,* Schmemann writes of the "task" of theology today:

> The task of theology in any given moment is necessarily determined by the needs of the Church, and the first task of the theologian is always to discern and to accept these needs, to become aware of what the Church expects from him.[11]

In a call to "recover the *pastoral* dimension ... that essential link between the Tradition of the Church and real life,"[12] Schmemann clearly speaks of such an application. Less than this is a "defect," and such a defect (again in which the "whole picture" is lost), comes from a divorce between theology and the real life of the Church:

> ... its [theology's] almost total divorce from the real life of the Church and from her *practical* needs ... the theologian is accustomed to looking at everything "practical" as virtually opposed to theology and its lofty pursuits ...[13]

Pointing to the Fathers of the Patristic age as examples of those who clearly saw how theology "engaged" real life, Schmemann says:

> And it is their constant, truly "existential" preoccupation with, and then total commitment to, salvation of real, concrete men that makes every line they wrote so ultimately serious and their theology so vital and precisely pastoral.[14]

[11]Alexander Schmemann, *Church, World, Mission* (Crestwood, NY: St Vladimir's Seminary Press, 1979) p. 118.
[12]*Ibid.,* p. 119.
[13]*Ibid.,* p. 120.
[14]*Ibid.,* p. 121.

This is, in Schmemann's words, a true contrast to a theology which "has become exclusively 'academic,' 'scholastic,' in the literal sense of the word," and which has been "confined to a narrow circle of professional intellectuals, writing and working, in fact, for each other."[15]

Thus, both extremes have persistently haunted this personal domain of the ministry to persons, as Leech aptly points to one (reductionism to certain problems, crises, etc.), and Schmemann to the other (a non-applicable, non-dialectical, "divorce" of theology from "real man").

Both warnings, in terms of our present task, lead us to one conclusion: this dimension of "ministry" must deal with the entire scope of the Christian life and growth of the person, which includes but certainly cannot be limited to, the various "knots," crises, problems, etc. that arise in that life. This is the balance which keeps direction and counselling solidly within the spiritual realm of "ministry."

In any era, then, the issues that come into a person's life, whether he is a victim of them or the cause of them, are solidly related to his entire spiritual life. In effect, the core issue—the true "spiritual" issue—which is missed in either aforementioned extreme, is what that person will make of these issues, whatever they may be. The question is not "will such issues and problems come or not," nor is it a question of circumventing them, nor even of "burying one's head in the sand"; they *will* come. But will the person *grow* from them? Will he confront them, integrate them, in order to transform them into causes for growth? Indeed, the issue, then, is spiritual growth in the ministry to persons; in many ways this is that quality which distinguishes the Christian ministry, and most particularly, the pastor's ministry to persons, from the many secular approaches to counselling. The pastor, especially, is there *to touch and to stretch* Christian persons; if he does not touch them first, he cannot stretch them; if he does not intend to stretch them, his touch has no ultimate purpose, has no true spiritual intent. The pastor, through such a "touch and stretch" orientation, is there to help persons to *choose to grow!* Both terms

[15]*Ibid.,* p. 120.

are crucial, *choice* and *growth,* so that when referring to growth, it is always inclusive of the person's capacity to choose that growth. In fact, as will be seen in the text that follows, there is no true growth without the person's free choice.

2. Growth: Theology for Ministry

What is the source of such an idea of "growth"? And why do we now purport that this is the final criterion, in whatever circumstance or problem arises, by which a true ministry to persons is measured? Even more, how is it that such a concept of "growth" holds together the "whole picture"? Some background is needed to understand the genesis of growth, an understanding which clearly shows how *theology* leads to *ministry.*

"Growth," as it is being here expressed, does not merely refer to a process of increasing "intellectualization," nor to an inherent mental capacity, nor even to an emotional matura- tion on the part of the person. Such qualities may be good in themselves in terms of knowing mathematics, geography, philosophy, or any kind of academic information. But here, growth is not to be limited to facts in any shape or form. A person can be, for example, "very intelligent" and still not grow, as we mean the term now. The same can be said about emotional maturation: a person can be emotionally mature and still not respond as a Christian, or still do evil things.

On the other hand, no one should naively assume that there is not a deep connection between the spiritual, and the psychological, physiological, sociological, etc. How a person thinks, perceives, and thus acts (which are psy- chological functions), is crucial to how the Christian lives. The spiritual *directs* the psychological, just as it does the physiological, the sociological, and in fact, all of life. The difference, which makes all the difference, is that growth— spiritual growth—as we mean it, takes a particular context: it is situated in the striving for "wholeness," or for "holiness" (both words are from the same root and truly mean the same: ὅλος—a "holding together") *within* oneself (heart and mind) and *between* oneself and others (God or the "least of the brethren"). Wherever thinking, acting, choosing—in fact any psychological, physiological or sociological functions—are involved in such a context, i.e. in the process of the person's *relationships,* they are important to his spiritual growth. A very clear example of the relationship between these two realms can be seen when we remember what happens in the Eucharist. The act of eating is a physiological (somatic) function. In the Eucharistic liturgy we "eat" (as well as see, hear, smell, etc.). It remains a physiological act, but now it becomes a question of the context and meaning of that function, of how one eats, what one eats, the spiritual disposition of the one who eats, i.e. precisely the final *meaning* of the act of eating. The context is clear in this case: the spiritual *directs* the physiological just as it does the psychological and sociological. Spirituality, in the end, has to do with "direction," in that it directs all that one does in his life toward, or away from, God (spirituality can be positive or negative). In this way, then, "spirituality" and spiritual growth, remain in a true dialectic relationship (and not a mere "philosophy") to the man who does think, act, and choose in his life. This is the context in which we place growth; this is the meaning of the "whole picture."

In truth, the concept of ministry for spiritual growth is rooted deeply in theology itself, and the ministry in response to that theology is rooted in what God himself has done and continues to do. We must very briefly, but also very clearly, summarize this theology before we proceed.

1. God created the world and humans (Adam and Eve) in his image and likeness.

2. In this state of primordial bliss, humans were innocent and simple; they were created "very good."

3. They had the possibility (potentiality) to remain in such a state, and to continue to grow into God's

presence, as long as they remained in communion
with God.

4. They broke this communion when, in pride, they
chose their "own way" and sinned, thus "falling"
from God.

5. However, the image of God was not obliterated,
but only marked, in this fall.

6. God's love, however, does not cease for them, and
thus he sends his Son Jesus Christ and the Holy
Spirit to restore humankind to the state of communion with him.

7. There remains a potential in all persons to grow
into communion with God, through his grace and
through their natural potential toward that growth.

What this means in terms of growth, is that a life lived
before God is not static, but *dynamic*. Choices can, and must,
be made. A *response* is called for in terms of how a person
lives with God and other human beings. The "goal" is
communion with God, but such communion requires that
choices be made—choices that deal with one's own world.

John Meyendorff emphasizes this point on the inborn and
dynamic nature of a person's growth in terms of a *goal* to
be reached. In this way he points to the ultimate meaning of
such a natural dynamic element, the "free movement toward
God" (which is never disconnected from the person's life in
this world).

> God not only grants beings their existence, and in the
> case of man, an eternal existence; but he also assigns
> to them a goal to reach, and in the case of man this
> goal implies a free movement toward God.[16]

With the concept of a "goal to reach," there is here a
true dynamic element, a growth element. Man by cooperating

[16]John Meyendorff, *Christ in Eastern Christian Thought* (Crestwood, NY:
St Vladimir's Seminary Press, 1975) p. 137.

with God, in communion with God, grows. This is in his very nature as a *potential*. Adam and Eve were thus not created *in actuality* perfect, but certainly *in potentiality*; otherwise, how could perfection sin? However, because this was only a potentiality, they had a choice to either realize this potentiality or not. Of course, in pride, they chose not to go the way of growth into God, and, as a result, became less than they were potentially created to be. As we have said, choice is an essential part of growth, and there is no true growth without this free choice. Thus, man was actually created to grow toward becoming his true self, i.e. a self in communion with God, by making the right choices. Georges Florovsky says it this way:

> Only in this "communion" with God does a man become "himself"; in separation from God and in self-isolation, on the contrary, he falls to a place lower than himself.[17]

But, if this is the theory, ministry asks of this theology: what is truly involved in man's reaching this "goal" (free movement toward God)? What is involved in truly being "in communion" with God? How is man to truly "become himself"? This is the point where the theology *guides* the ministry, and where the ministry *realizes* the theology. This must be our present concern.

What we have just presented is but a brief summary of the theology of growth, now given only in order to set the context for our present concern. In the end, the major concern of both ministry and theology is, and has always been, one of *Theosis* (or the reaching of "God-like-ness" of humankind) into which a person grows through his choices regarding both God and other persons.

The point here for "ministry" is that the person is endowed with *choice,* and, with the *right* choice(s), the possibility of *growth*; choice because God created him with free will, growth because God implanted a dynamic and expansive element in his nature. As we shall see, this aspect of choice is crucial in the ministry to persons. The person can, of course, choose incorrectly, wrongly, immorally. He can grow in an aberrant direction, away from God. In either case he will not "grow into his true self."

This element of growth is the basis on which the pastoral counselor works in any of the areas of direction and counsel. His faith in the goodness of God and his creation colors his direction and makes it positive and affirmative. He believes that the person's potential goodness is God's original plan, even if that person is "fallen" in his sin, and chooses wrongly. This theological truth "cuts into" the lives of persons who are found today by the pastor or Christian counselor, whether in a particular crisis or not. If this theology does not "cut into" life, then in fact it remains a philosophy, having nothing to do with how Christian humans live before God. (In such a case Alexander Schmemann's earlier warning is absolutely correct.)

3. Spiritual Growth and the Pastoral Effort

For the pastor in his ministry to persons, therefore, the unfortunate truth which places this theology of growth (*Theosis*) into the dynamics of human life is this: although God created the person with goodness ("very good") and with a natural capacity to grow into himself, this does *not mean that he will!* Thus, the theology becomes the core of the ministry: human choices must be made, and the "Great Deceiver"—the Devil himself—works continually to influence those choices. The effort of the pastor must concentrate on such choices and the various dynamics which cluster around them. It cannot be forgotten that these choices are every-day, every-minute, "normal" circumstances, choices which the Christian person makes regarding self and others.

William Oglesby in *Biblical Themes for Pastoral Care* presents certain "themes" from scripture that are relevant to the effort of the pastoral counselor. Each theme deals ultimately with the growth of persons through the exploration of the dynamics of choice. Oglesby paints the picture of three orientations, each of which is important to how a person chooses under the counsel of the pastor: *insight, behavior,* and *being.*

> Although these three illustrations are presented in the barest of sketches, the underlying presuppositions . . . . are nonetheless relevant to the task of ministry. It is evident that all three are genuinely concerned with "right-knowing" (insight-orientation), "right-doing" (behavior-orientation), and "right-being" (personal transformation).[18]

Oglesby's claim is that of the three, it is the third, "right-being," which is the crucial orientation, and from this emerge the first two: "right-knowing" and "right-doing."

> It is evident that the Bible sees all three concepts as important. Indeed, there is a sense in which the whole story of God's revelation and human response can be told in terms of knowing, doing and being. The crucial question . . . is which of these is seen as primary and which derivative.[19]

In the ministry to persons, the pastoral counselor must eventually "minister" precisely on this third level—"right-being." Oglesby's points regarding the limitation of the first two are good ones: neither "insight" (which is where most secular therapies end) nor "doing" (which is where secular "behaviorists" end) go far enough, *if* they are considered ends in themselves. Rather, they derive from "right-being." In turn, "right-being" is the deepest orientation since it clearly has to do with the "heart." The pastoral counselor knows that the person must have a "change of heart" in order to grow spiritually. It is the heart which deals with "being relationships," both with God and man (cf. Mt

[18]William Oglesby, *Biblical Themes for Pastoral Care* (Nashville, Tenn.: Abingdon, 1980) p. 18.
[19]*Ibid.,* p. 25.

5:8, Mk 7:21-23, Rom 6:17 and Ja 4:8, as well as many Old Testament sources). "Citations can be multiplied, but it is evident that quality of life (being, heart) is primary to quality of thought and quality of behavior."[20]

If the counselor is to lead a person to true growth, it must penetrate to the level of the "heart," at the level of his "being." This is true since his real choices, i.e. his *life*-choices regarding God and man, are made "from the heart," and it is upon those right choices that he grows, so that ultimately his "being" is one with God.

> So it is that pastoral care... (which focuses on *being* without disregarding *knowing* and *doing*) is consistent with the biblical perspective, which sees all three as essential, but also is clear on the basic priority of being over knowing and doing. The three attitudinal intentions of helping involve three words: "I instruct you" (*didasco*), "I urge you" (*parakalo*) and "I love you" (*agapao*) ... there can be no doubt that the primary word is *agapao*.[21]

But it is also at this deep "being" level of the heart (to which Orthodox spirituality is always pointing as the central issue), where many negative "blocks" to growth can be seen; such "blocks" are in the very practical dynamics of a person's life, and they are true challenges to the pastor's counsel of his flock. There are many factors which serve to "block" spiritual growth, some self-imposed, some other-imposed. *Theosis* serves as a goal which calls "ordinary" persons—not only ascetic fathers—to think, act, and choose in a certain way. Thus the pastoral effort must deal with these "blocks," which every pastor has seen, e.g. between two persons, in a marriage, in a family, with in-laws, with neighbors or fellow workers, in the parish community, etc. And they can indeed exist at the deepest level of being, emerging in fact "from the heart."

One "block" to a proper growth, for example, is ex-

[20]*Ibid.*, p. 29.
[21]*Loc. cit.*

pressed by Alexander Elchaninov, who warns of the error of always expecting "flawless achievements," either from ourselves or others, and in which we become easily "irritated" and even fall into "despair."

> Typical of the errors which lead to depression, to wrong evaluations, is ... the idea that here on earth ... there can be flawless achievements on our part, and on the part of other men, in our human relationships. Consequently we expect of ourselves the perfection of sanctity and are disheartened when, in our holiest moments, we discover in our hearts impurity, vainglory, duplicity; we are irritated when men we had considered flawless prove to be cowardly, malicious, untruthful; we despair when we see in God's own Church schisms, disputes, jealousies, envy—the unleashing storm of human passions. And yet "such things must needs be" (Mk 13:7); the entire world is infected with sin; the terrible fissure runs through it from top to bottom. If ... among Christ's disciples, there was a Judas, why be shocked? Every parish has its lesser Judas, but it also has its meek, "spirit bearing" John, its faithful, active Peter.[22]

How true this is! This is an honest beginning for the pastor. But beside this truth, there is also the truth, stated by St Gregory of Nyssa, that human nature is "mutable and prone to change" (otherwise there could be no growth), in contrast to God who is "permanent and immutable." The hope which a person has, in fact, is built upon this dynamic capacity to "change" (for the better!) and thereby to truly grow. Here Nyssa is also very hopeful and adds to what Elchaninov is saying:

> But in truth the finest aspect of our mutability is the possibility of growth in good; and this capacity for

[22]Alexander Elchaninov, *The Diary of a Russian Priest* Crestwood, NY: St Vladimir's Seminary Press, 1982) p. 51.

improvement transforms the soul, as it changes, more and more into the divine.[23]

Therefore, the pastor must know that if he is to lead persons to true growth, he must recognize that the *good* and *bad* are part of this life: good, because God created the good; bad, not because God created anything bad, but because good is distorted by human beings and becomes bad. But one needs to deal with both, "discerning" constantly. Abba Evagrius of the Desert Fathers says it simply: "The good and bad that we meet in life can aid both virtues and vices. It is the task of good judgment to use them to further the first, i.e. virtue, and to frustrate the second, i.e. vices."[24]

The basis for the proper choice ("to further the first and to frustrate the second") is the ability to discern, to judge, to be aware—and these are functions of the Christian consciousness (conscience), without which no pastoral counselor can begin to lead persons to growth. The movement, then, is *from discernment to choice.*

John of Kronstadt adds:

The Lord allows the enemy to tempt us in order to prove us, in order to strengthen our spiritual powers in our struggle against the enemy, and so that we ourselves may see more clearly towards what our heart inclines, whether it inclines to patience, hope, and love and in general to virtue; or to irritability, murmuring, blasphemy, malice, and despair. Therefore, we must not be despondent, but must good-humoredly and patiently bear spiritual darkness that descends upon our soul, the fire that weakens and inclines us to impatience and malice, to affliction and oppression, knowing that all these are indispensable in the order of our spiritual life, that by these the Lord is proving us. Do not let us blaspheme against the true way—the way of holy faith and virtue, and

[23]St Gregory Nyssa, *From Glory to Glory,* ed. by Danielou and Musurillo (Crestwood, NY: St Vladimir's Seminary Press, 1979) pp. 83-84.
[24]Evagrius Ponticus, *The Praktikos* (Kalamazoo, MI, 1978) No. 88, p. 38.

do not let us prefer the evil way. We are free, and
must strengthen ourselves by every means and with
all our power in faith and virtue, unto the laying
down of our life for the way of truth; and how can
this be if we have no temptation?[25]

It is clear in Kronstadt's words: we are tempted in order
to "prove ourselves" and to transform, by free choice, *the
bad into the good*. Temptation, in fact, may "strengthen"
us, as he notes. The pastor must direct persons to see
this truth and to discern that such happenings, crises, or
circumstances which afflict us are not merely accidental; they
may in fact be precisely given by God so as to "prove" us.
Making this same point, Elchaninov says: "nothing in life
is accidental. Whoever believes in accident does not believe
in God."[26]

In such cases, where good and bad (in any of its forms)
comes, whether within a person or between persons, good
must come out of bad. Here "growth" means a true trans-
formation in which the bad is turned into a benefit, in which
the crisis is actually used to enable growth. But for this to
happen—and here the guidance of the pastor is essential—a
"spiritual warfare" is required, in which (through a proper
ministry to persons) one can be led to growth through
"labor and activity." One does not "sit back" in a slothful,
"woe-is-me!" manner, falling into self-pity:

Therefore labour and activity are indispensable for all.
Life without activity is not life, but something mon-
strous—a sort of phantom of life. This is why it is
the duty of every man to fight continually and persistently against slothfulness. "Unto everyone that
hath shall be given, and he shall have abundance;
but from him that hath not, shall be taken away even
that which he hath."[27]

This does not mean, however, that in the pastoral effort

[25]John Sergieff, *My Life in Christ* (Jordanville, NY, 1957) p. 58.
[26]*Op. cit.,* Elchaninov, p. 101.
[27]*Op. cit.,* Sergieff, p. 129.

to lead persons to spiritual growth, the pastor can forget his own limitations and humanity; indeed, he has nothing to give others which he has not first received from God. Continuous with all that has previously been said in this study, the priest remains God's instrument, who even in his humanity, is a *mediator,* acting in behalf of the "sole mediator" who is Christ:

> God has not made the angels who are holy . . . to be your mediators . . . but men who, like you, are burdened with weaknesses and sins and who, therefore, are indulgent to your weaknesses and errings which are the same in you as in them.[28]

The Desert Fathers also warn the priest not to forget his own human limitation, and thus, his own capacity for sinfulness:

> A brother who had sinned was turned out of the church by the priest; Abba Bessarion got up and went with him, saying "I too, am a sinner."[29]

This warning is further carried by a wonderful story from the Desert Fathers:

> A brother at Scetis committed a fault. A council was called to which Abba Moses was invited, but he refused to go to it. Then the priest sent someone to say to him, "Come, for everyone is waiting for you." So he got up and went. He took a leaking jug, filled it with sand and carried it with him. The others came out to meet him and said to him, "What is this, Father?" The old man said to them, "My sins run out behind me, and I do not see them, and today I am coming to judge the errors of another." When they heard that, they said no more to the brother but forgave him.[30]

[28]Bishop Alexander, *Father John of Kronstadt* (Crestwood, NY: St Vladimir's Seminary Press, 1979) p. 57.
[29]*Op. cit.,* Ward, p. 42
[30]*Ibid.,* p. 138.

Finally, Abba Dorotheos of Gaza says:

> And because of your own weakness, have sympathy
> with your brother and give thanks that you have
> found a starting place for forgiveness, that you may
> be forgiven by God for your many and greater faults.[31]

Through all his efforts in ministering to persons at this
deep "being-level" of the heart, the pastoral counselor cannot forget that he is working with a "gift of God" which
is implanted in the very nature of that person. His role is
to help the person rediscover this "gift," through any crisis,
problem, evil, etc. by "turning his mind to it" (to use St
Gregory of Nyssa's words) by leading him to "choose" to
look for it:

> ... the gift of God is not separated from our nature
> nor is it far from those who choose to look for it. . .
> It dwells within us, ignored and forgotten, "choked
> with the cares and pleasures of life" (Lk 8:14), but is
> rediscovered when we turn our minds to it.[32]

The pastor, then, is working upon what is already there
as potential (the "gift of God which is not separated from
our nature") but is now darkened by wrong choices, pride,
sin, resentment, jealousy or envy. What must be realistically
remembered is that *a person's nature and his choices must
be distinguished*! St Gregory says it this way:

> By our human efforts we can merely clear away the
> accumulated filth of sin and thus allow the hidden
> beauty of the soul to shine forth.[33]

and then he adds:

> The soul's divine beauty, that had been an imitator

[31]*Dorotheos of Gaza: Discourses and Sayings,* ed. E. Rozanne Elder,
Cistercian Studies Series (Kalamazoo, 1977) [Trans. Eric Wheeler] p. 238.
[32]*Op. cit., From Glory to Glory.*
[33]*Ibid.,* p. 114.

of its archetype, was, like a blade, darkened with the rust of sin.[34]

This positive and hopeful concept in which the soul is to be "an imitator of its archetype," can be realized by removing the rust of sin—which is another way of saying removing the "blocks"—in order to see the shine of the blade. Such a concept is expressed time and again by the Fathers, e.g. St John of Damascus in his *De Fide* and St Gregory Nazianzen in his *Oration 45*. The point is that the ministry to persons is oriented towards this *hopeful and positive* basis: that persons are created *by nature* very good (not *by choice*, i.e. they may still choose wrong, which in fact means that they are choosing "against their nature"!). This means that such persons will grow to where they belong through spiritual warfare and guidance, for they have the natural resources given by God, within themselves to do so. This is the basis for true growth in the life of the Christian person.

4. Out of Sickness and Sin

In the ministry of spiritual counsel, then, the pastor's aim is to deal honestly with the various "blocks," in order to lead persons toward spiritual growth. The theological roots of such a hopeful outlook are present and inborn, giving true hope in any situation which may develop. Whether or not the pastor is constantly conscious of this hope, it still belies his perspective in his care for persons. His faith, which is never neutral, will continuously be interpreting both the circumstance and direction of the person.

A particular development brought before every pastor, and which calls for special direction within the ministry to persons, is the presence of *sickness and sin.* Spiritual growth must again be the goal in this minstry.

First, that sickness and sin are related has always been known. Psalm 38 captures this intimate relationship:

[34]*Ibid.,* p. 113.

O Lord, rebuke me not in thy anger, nor chasten me
in thy wrath!... There is no soundness in my flesh
because of thy indignation; there is no health in my
bones because of my sin. For my iniquities have gone
over my head; they weigh like a burden too heavy
for me...I am utterly bowed down and prostrate;
all the day I go about mourning. For my loins are
filled with burning, and there is no soundness in my
flesh. I am utterly spent and crushed; I groan because
of the tumult of my heart...My heart throbs, my
strength fails me; and the light of my eyes—it also is
gone from me.

Like the Psalmist, St Cyril of Alexandria speaks of the
relationship of sickness and sin:

Human nature became sick with sin...the many became sinners, not because they transgressed together
with Adam (for they were not there), but because of
his nature which entered under the dominion of sin...
Human nature became ill and subject to corruption
through the transgression of Adam, thus, penetrating
·man's very passions.[35]

Both the Psalmist and St Cyril are stating the universal
and cosmical truth, known in theology, that sickness and
its final terminus, death, has broken in upon all of life
through sin. For them it is clear: the "sin of Adam" leads
to the entrance of sickness in all its forms. This does not
mean, in a personal causal sense, that every child who
suffers a sickness, does so because of some "sin" of his own
(more on this will follow).

It can also be said that sin is itself the "sickness of
humankind" in that sin breaks communion with God, and
a person without communion with God is, in this sense,
"sick." A most accurate description of a sickness is whenever one is "not himself," i.e. he is suffering from a
"dis-ease," i.e. he is not "at ease" with himself and God.

[35]St Cyril of Alexandria, *On Romans 5:18* in Migne P.G. 74, 789.

For such a sickness, it is confession after a true repentance that is the healing therapy. (In this way the Fathers often called the sacraments "medicine.")

But beside this universal, cosmical relationship, every pastor has seen a most personal and particular relationship within the dynamics of a person's life, in two directions: from sin to sickness, and from sickness to sin. When he sees this happening, the pastor must honestly deal with it. For example, when the dynamic moves *from sin to sickness,* the results are both physical (somatic) and emotional. The sin is normally felt through a guilty conscience and leads to anxiety, anguish, scrupulosity, despair, etc. which, in turn, easily become somatic formations, e.g. ulcers, headaches, physical withdrawal, isolation, nervousness, etc.

When the dynamic moves *from sickness to sin,* a physical ailment can lead to bitterness, envy, suspicion, resentment, anger, depression, etc. It does not, of course, have to be this way, nor should it even be this way. But it is found constantly by the pastor in his ministry to persons, and again, he must see his counsel within such circumstances as leading to the possibility for growth. In such circumstances both the *physical* and *emotional* results of sin and sickness must be examined.

5. The Implications of Physical (Somatic) Sickness

It should first be understood that there are always volitional components to the physical sickness of the person. In the true "spiritual" sense, what becomes important in the ministry of counsel is what the person believes and thus will make of this physical ailment. Without such an understanding no growth will occur.

We can take the example of the person who has an incurable disease. On the part of the helping pastor, this takes not only a narrow somatic interpretation, since that person has the "spiritual" problem of what he will *make* of it; either his faith (toward God) or his bitterness (away from God) may increase. Who will help this person *discern* in such a way, if not the pastor? Is this not a case of "antecedent faith" in which the event is interpreted by the faith? Can this be what Jesus meant in St Mark: "For to him who has, will more be given; and from him who has not, even what he has shall be taken away" (Mk 4:25). We see here that the fundamental task for the pastor is still one of "faith" which meets and interprets the events of life.

Thus, when the physical dimension *is* involved, the pastor must not only look for and pray for—healing in the narrow sense, but also for finding *meaning* in that physical disease; this is true, even when we pray and anoint for a *cure* of the physical ailment. (We see here that anointing has also a "consecratory" aspect.) Furthermore, at this point the paradigm of Lazarus also speaks: Lazarus was healed, physically being raised from the dead, but he still had to die. The ministry to persons in the physical sense, then, *includes but can never be limited to,* the somatic cure of the ailment.

With such an interpretation—which the pastoral counselor can best give—we find no chemical, medicinal interpretation, as important as that may be in itself. Nor do we find any "magical" or "charismatic" reaction. Instead there is here the entrance of *meaning* into existence, and it is this quality, i.e. meaning, that the pastor brings, and thus, also a perspective for true growth.

This works when we see that, in terms of human experience, healing aims to bring each of these experiences into the larger questions of meaning. This the pastor does as he leads another to discover that, in the middle of my *problem,* can be the meaning of my *existence.* Here, indeed, the "whole picture" is preserved. As quoted in *Orthodox Synthesis,* "wherever we begin with human problems we recognize that what we see and feel here and now, may *break open* for us at any time questions concerning the meaning of our existence."[36] The introduction of one's relationship with God, i.e. "the meaning of our existence," into the search for such healing is not arbitrary, but is its very foundation.

[36]In *Orthodox Synthesis,* ed. Joseph Allen (Crestwood, NY: St Vladimirs Seminary Press, 1981) p. 218ff. This particular section on the physical implications is found in more detail in this source.

This directly relates healing to real spiritual growth. Of course, healing does not, fortunately, always depend upon our understanding of its sources; it is God who heals regardless of the consciousness of the mediator. This the pastor must proclaim continuously.

Furthermore, this is also true because man is both "whole and parts," i.e. his whole life, as a well as his arm, his leg, his stomach—every part of his life and experience is connected with every other part. There is no incident in his personal history which may not be reflected in the direction of his whole being. Have we not seen or read this many times in history? "A trivial incident may open the way for the first time to the discovery of oneself and God."[37] Can this be what St Paul means: "for this slight momentary affliction is preparing for us an *eternal* weight of glory beyond all comparison (2 Cor 4:17). A somatic illness may become the way—sometimes, unfortunately, the *only* way—that we face the ultimate issues of life. The struggle within ourselves as a result of the somatic illness, may bring into clear focus how we must struggle for spiritual growth towards God. Somatically, a recovery from an illness can reflect the goodness of God. These are all examples of "healing" as the reconciliation of our present experience with the meaning of our existence. Of course, one can never know beforehand exactly when this type of connection, i.e. of the part to the whole, will take place. But each incident may precisely lead someone to face those issues that go to the roots of his life. This is a true "growth," and it is this possibility which the pastor must keep alive for the person.

In relation with this is another growth issue. The pastor must keep this concept of meaning alive, even in the face of those somatic illnesses which may *never* be removed from the person's life. The real growth, in this case, may come just at that point where such limitations are acknowledged and are integrated into that person's courageous acceptance. "The Lord gave, and the Lord has taken away; blessed be the name of the Lord" (Job 1:21). In short, the limitation,

[37] *Ibid.*, p. 220.

whatever it be, may be that very door through which one walks into the arena where ultimate questions are asked and answered.

Each situation which can be presented, then, can be an example of how the disease or suffering itself can be used for growth. Here the prayer of Pascal makes real sense: "Thou didst give me health that I may serve Thee, and I put it all to worldly use. Now Thou sendest me sickness to correct me; let me not use it to avoid Thee through my impatience."[38] Other meanings, then, besides those immediate somatic ones, must be discovered if the pastor will effectively lead the person toward growth.

6.   The Implications of Emotional Sickness

Like the physical implications just mentioned, the pastor must also be aware of certain emotional sicknesses (disturbances) which may be forthcoming in a person's life—from sin or otherwise. It has already been said that, here, the goal is not "good mental health," nor "emotional maturation," as such, although a proper "spirituality" will normally manifest itself in these ways; this again, is to be seen in the context of the "whole picture," to which the earlier warnings of Leech and Schmemann pointed. Whether one refers to "just government," to "honest economics," to "emotional well-being," etc., is never the ending point, the final meaning. However, the *true* final meaning—the context of man before God and neighbor—will always color each choice made in "this world." This means that the human world is not to be bypassed, but is to be judged and determined by this context. A stable, emotional well-being, therefore, is not the source, nor even the purpose, but the *fruit* of a proper spirituality.

Alexander Elchaninov realizes that this must be a personal concern for the pastor in his ministry to others. He makes his point to the pastor in *Diary of a Russian Priest*:

[38]Paul Tournier, *A Doctor's Casebook in Light of the Bible* (New York: Harper and Row, 1976) p. 201.

You cannot cure the soul of others or help people without having changed yourself. You cannot put in order the spiritual economy of others, so long as there is chaos in your own soul. You cannot bring peace to others if you do not have it yourself.[39]

Elchaninov knows that a person who is disturbed suffers precisely from an "inner chaos," from an enslavement to any kind of "passion" which has him out of order and in "disease." He cannot judge and discern—he cannot *choose* correctly—and because he is listening to, and enslaving himself to such subjective passions, his emotional life loses a "proper economy." So, "to free ourselves from inner chaos, we must recognize *objective* order."[40]

The beginning of the spiritual life is to emerge from subjectivity from oneself, to outgrow oneself by entering into communion with the highest principle—with God.[41]

Like the ascetic fathers, Elchaninov understands what the pastor must do regarding this emotional component in the person's life. He does not mean that growth requires a "gnawing self-analysis," nor a "morbid self-flagellation," nor even a prideful "concentration on ourselves." Rather, he means an

attentive, calm survey of the soul, a gaze turned inward, a deliberate effort to build up our lives consciously; so that we are not carried away by every passing emotion and idea. We are not in the slightest degree our own masters. We need practice, the discipline of attentive and determined work upon ourselves.[42]

Who but the pastor can bring—as he does in the physical realm—such a perspective: "a calm survey of the soul, a

[39]*Ibid.*, Elchaninov, *The Diary*, p. 218.
[40]*Ibid.*, p. 34.
[41]*Ibid.*, p. 99.
[42]*Ibid.*, p. 175.

gaze turned inward," in order to reach communion with God and man?

Thus, this experienced pastor knows that the Christian counselor, in order to properly minister to persons, must be aware of such emotional implications: "Every priest must be well informed about nervous and psychic diseases; this is absolutely necessary in pastoral practice."[43] Reflecting Psalm 38, his wish for the pastor to realize such implications within the person's spiritual life, comes because

> ... often ... a painful condition of the soul, weighed down by sin, entangled and confused by unresolved conflicts, is mistaken for nervous disease.[44]

How very difficult it is for such persons, thus trapped by this particular type of "block," to remember that God can still forgive them if there is true repentance. Such a person thinks he has sins "too great" to be forgiven; his confession will never be received by God, it will never be "perfect" enough. His scrupulosity conditions him: "How *could* I receive the sacraments?"; God's grace cannot be accepted by him. He easily forgets that no person is truly worthy: "We have done no good deed ..." as St Paul said. Thomas Hopko warns of such an aberration that leads even to "mental and spiritual disorder," when the person forgets the *faith* issue of forgiveness, "If God is for us, who is against us?" (Rom 8:31):

> There are never so many or so great sins that God is not able to forgive them. There is never a confession so perfect that it merits God's mercy because of its perfection. There is never a Holy Communion which is not both given and received by a sinner. Any other thought on any of these points is not only bad theology, but blasphemy; and could even lead to mental and spiritual disorder.[45]

[43]*Ibid.*, p. 213.
[44]*Ibid.*, p. 213.
[45]Thomas Hopko, *If We Confess Our Sins* (Syosset, NY: Orthodox Church in America, Dept. of Religious Education, 1975) p. 36.

The simple truth is that when a person has guilt, he either *punishes* himself—or he *changes*! If he "holds on" to the sin (and guilt is the way that one "holds on"), self-punishment is a way to avoid growth (through change). It is only by repentance, by the person's willingness to surrender to God's grace and forgiveness (which is always available in the person's sincerity) that true freedom comes and brings with it true growth.

Thus, in terms of the person's emotional life within this "whole picture," one of the most important happenings which occurs when he comes to the pastor (especially, but not solely, in Confession) is that the person can get his self-image out before himself, thereby seeing it for what it truly is, i.e. self-interpretation through other-interpretation. What is false and sinful in his self-image, what is grandiose, prideful? Where is the discrepancy between what he *is* and *pretends to be?* On the other hand, when does one slothfully become "satisfied," forgetting that he is never totally defined by what he is, but by what he desires to become.

Here the role of the pastor is obvious. He is someone trusted, to whom one can disclose his "self" with all his sins, someone before whom he can "die" in this way. And, even more, the pastor represents God and the Church! When one talks with the pastor, that person can hear what he himself is *saying.* Furthermore, the pastor can help that person to *interpret* what he is really saying. What "idols" has he created in order to avoid coming to grips with himself? What "idols" has he created that keep him from the painful truth about what is truly required in order for him to "co-operate" (*synergy*) with God? What is needed for any change—and thus growth—in each case, is a *reordering of our self-image,* and it must be a constant re-ordering (i.e. a continuing growth.) It is this very personal relationship and communion with the pastor which can release a person and thus lead to such growth, both within himself and between himself and the other.

But throughout, we have attempted to make this clear: because such growth is at the "being" level of the heart, this is no simple task in the ministry to persons. Alexander

Elchaninov speaks of how persons use their "intelligence and imagination," in fact, to *avoid* such growth by creating a whole "wardrobe of masks and costumes":

> These are like larvae—they stifle the original kernel of personality and multiply, covering it with a parasitic growth. Hence the complexity, entanglements, inevitable falsifications and loss of personality.[46]

In terms of the ministry of spiritual counsel, it is the pastor who gently, firmly, and with love, can help another realize that "the self-image is never *only* a self-image."[47] Immanence and transcendance can never be separated; we know who we are when we discover to Whom we belong. "It is no longer I who live, but Christ who lives in me" (Gal 2:20). Can there ever be a self-understanding apart from some grasp of origin and destiny? It is the pastor who can best represent that world with which the person must come to terms, i.e. who can bear the truth about life which must be grasped.

Finally, in keeping within the realm of growth as a natural quality given by God to the Christian person, even if and when that growth is "blocked by the rust," Elchaninov says the following:

> Only through strenuous effort will the true personality discover itself among all these parasites and find its way through this noisy, motley crowd. One may destroy these parasites by despising and ignoring them and by limiting the sphere of one's interests. But it is almost impossible to achieve this without the aid of a friend or a priest, for real personality can be so stifled and suppressed that its rediscovery offers the greatest difficulties; the inexperienced prefer the risk of giving new strength to their own larvae. The usual

---

[46]*Op. cit.,* Elchaninov, p. 64.

[47]Daniel Williams, *The Minister and Care of the Soul* (New York: Harper and Row, 1961) p. 14.

result of this is a muddled life, a wrongly chosen profession; in the worst cases, insanity.[48]

In the ministry of counsel, then, the pastoral counselor is indeed present to introduce persons to themselves, to their *true* selves. This represents growth.

[48]*Op. cit.*, Elchaninov, p. 64.

CHAPTER EIGHT

Spiritual Growth
and the Secular World

The final consideration in the ministry of spiritual counsel
has to do with the question of the secular world in which
the contemporary Christian person lives. The aim of the
pastor or Christian counselor in guiding persons remains
one of growth, but now the task must be viewed in light of:
(1) the kind of world which is present, i.e. "what is there?"
and then, (2) the proper pastoral response in light of
that world.

1. Growth and Secularity

To minister to persons, to lead them to growth as we
have proposed, means that one needs to understand and to
deal with—to confront—the world in which such persons live.
"What is there?" one must ask. It is clear that the contemporary atmosphere is one of secularity, and this is described
in many ways.

Langdon Gilkey, in his book *Naming the Whirlwind: The
Renewal of God-Language,* seeks to explain contemporary
secularism in terms of its pervasive influence upon literature,
art, music, philosophy, and even, religion. His point is that
to exist in an age is to be influenced by its spirit:

When we speak . . . of the "spirit," "mind," "mood,"

201

or "Geist" of our culture, we refer to that deep preconceptual attitude toward, and understanding of, existence which dominates and forms the cultural life of an epoch, the way men of a given time characteristically apprehend the world they live in and their place within it; their fundamental self-understanding of their being in the world.[1]

Naturally, the manner in which persons "apprehend the world they live in," the way they come to understand "their being in the world," has a great impact upon the kind of task the pastoral counselor has with the person. As we have said earlier (in reference to growth, to any of the particular "blocks," to "sin and sickness," to the being-level of the heart, etc.), the challenge of the contemporary setting is that such factors must be encountered *within* this pervasive world-view of the person's existence. The very thought-forms, and even the language, which persons use to make their judgments or choices, must themselves be challenged.

The problem is revealed, for example, when the pastor finds himself asking, "where are the committed believers?" The answer is that they are there, but:

They are swimming against the tide. The dominant current of our culture, rather than supporting them as it would have in the past, threatens to submerge them.[2]

It is true that, at one time, the philosophy of the culture supported certain "religious principles," even if the reality did not live up to it. This "break" between the philosophy and the actions of the person has always been true, especially in the Western world. There was, thus, a tension which existed between the "is" and the "ought." However, in this secular world-view, even that tension seems to be gone:

It is perfectly respectable to be non-religious, and in

[1] Langdon Gilkey, *Naming the Whirlwind: The Renewal of God-Language* (Indianapolis, Inc. and N.Y. Bobbs-Merrill, 1969) p. 3.
[2] Frances Tyrrell, *Man: Believer and Unbeliever* (New York: Alba, 1974) p. 43.

certain circles, especially among the intellectuals, it is quite disreputable or at least eccentric to be anything else. It would appear that we are fast approaching ... the situation ... where believers pursue their distinctive commitments on the fringes, rather than at the heart of the world in which they live.[3]

The natural conclusion is that this secular world-view, or *vision,* becomes an "ethic" of sorts. One can speak of such an ethic as taking many shapes, expressed in many schools of thought: "naturalism," "materialism," "humanism," etc. But whichever form a secular ethic takes, its source, and the goals which are set, are drawn from *human experience alone.* Faith in God, in his revealed purposes, in his judgments, etc., has no place in directly formulating this ethic. Consequently, the thrust of such an "ethic" generally ends with whatever fosters human development: wiping out poverty, good relations between nations, proper mental health, better education, etc.

Such goals in themselves might also be desired by Christians. But positive as they may be—or the fact that such goals are shared—does not mean that the reasons for holding them are the same! What becomes a distinct problem, in terms of the ministry, is that there is no standard of judgment in the secular world-view. Secularists speak of the human experience, but experience is hardly a source of moral judgment because it is "neutral," is neither good nor bad in itself; one experiences "good and bad" things. In other words, one's experience is merely a "receiver"—to be sure, the deepest receiver—but something else must judge both what it receives and what it does with what it receives. Having no absolutes, then, such an "ethic" finally comes to mean that what was "immoral" one hundred years ago (or perhaps one hundred years hence) is not immoral today. This is the consequence when there is nothing but human experience.

Therefore, in a secular world where persons are ministered to, there is no doctrine or belief which would be

[3]*Loc. cit.,* p. 43.ft

normative for judgment, or for the formation of conscience. The guidelines which existed in pre-secular ages, are irrelevant in such a world; they have no real value to persons today, or at best, they exist but belong in a category that does not truly relate to their life. And it must immediately be said that to pretend, in the contemporary ministry, that this is not so for the Christian person also, is just that: pretending.

Does this render the pastor helpless in the secular age? Absolutely not! In fact, one must live in but be not *of* the world. In order to guide persons to growth, therefore, the *Christian consciousness* itself must be touched by the contemporary pastor. Robert Lauder stresses the necessity of this because of the prevailing *secular* consciousness of the world:

> They (Christians) must try to preserve and defend their faith among contemporaries whose consciousness has been colored. Simply put, secular humanism is in the air. Even among those who never read its philosophers, perhaps never even heard of them, the secularistic vision has taken root. It is not necessary that contemporary people be aware of the meaning of the expression "secular humanism"; but they are being bombarded by it nevertheless.[4]

The meanings and values which secularism presents have become dominant; thus, the spiritual counsel must penetrate to that same depth. How can this be done?

For the pastor who must deal with such a deeply set secular world-view, it is not enough to merely describe or to denounce it. One must go through and beyond such a worldview to build—or rather *re*-build—a *network of Christian meanings* which will penetrate deeply enough into the level of the consciousness of the person. The Fathers of the Church use various words to describe this quality of consciousness: "apperception," "awareness," "discernment"— even "conscience" itself. It is only from the deepest level of

---

[4]Robert Lauder, *The Priest as Person* (Whitinsville, Mass.: Affirmation Books, 1981) p. 26.

consciousness that the person will be able to realize values, to make his judgments, and in turn, to act upon them.

To accomplish such a difficult task, the pastor must deal with those aspects which comprise such a network. Three aspects are most important: *the fixing of new faith horizons, freedom,* and *truth.*

2. Fixing New Faith Horizons in the Secular World

In order to build this network of Christian meanings, the pastor must help the person to establish a proper "faith horizon." Jesus himself is constantly calling persons to horizons which set new meanings, and he does this immediately *within their present circumstances.* In each case, our Lord is truly calling for a new level of consciousness.

> In almost every Gospel scene, Jesus tries to offer new meaning to people. He calls people to enter a new world, to expand their horizons, to accept a new set of meanings.[5]

One clear example of this is in the teaching of the Beatitudes. With this proclamation in that sermon, Christ turns the then current faith values "upside down."

> On several important points, he gives his listeners a new vision of how people should act and what is important in human life, e.g. that they should love their enemies and do good to those who hate them. In the sixth chapter of Luke, Jesus' recitation of the beatitudes follows two scenes revealing the Pharisees' excessive legalism (in which he turns the "legal" virtues upside down) ... Clearly Jesus is trying to expand the horizons of his listeners, and Luke is trying to expand the horizons of his readers.[6]

Our Lord does this often; a second example is when he

[5]*Ibid.,* p. 41.
[6]*Ibid.,* p. 43.

deals with the Samaritan Woman (Jn 4:7-30). "At least
five times Jesus tries to expand the Samaritan woman's
horizon, to call her beyond herself into a new world."[7] He
does this, first, in merely asking her for a drink of water
(the Jews and Samaritans had no communication); secondly,
in his response, "If you knew the gift of God, and who it
is that is saying to you, 'Give me a drink,' you would have
asked him, and he would have given you living water";
thirdly, in reference to the "living water," she makes the
most trite comment that "you have nothing to draw with";
fourthly, in his revelation that she has had five husbands
(in response to a comment which has nothing at all to do
with "husbands"); fifthly, in his response to the "place"
of worship, "neither on this mountain nor in Jerusalem."
In all this Jesus expands her horizons, which then turn her
presupposed values "upside down," ending, of course, with
the ultimate truth: "I am he." Then comes the recognition
on her part: "Can this be the Christ?"

These examples are not disconnected from the efforts
of the contemporary pastor in dealing with persons in the
secular world; he too must turn the world "upside down."
The pastor must ask himself constantly, in relation to the
person's life (whether in a particular crisis or not), what
horizons *is* he setting for the person? Is he calling the person
at all? And if he is, what sources is he using to set such
horizons? This, again, enables spiritual "growth." This effort is only to "make present" those qualities and values
that have always been preserved by the Christian faith, but
have been "dulled" by secularity: truth, commitment, love,
hope, etc. Making these meanings present—or even more,
dominant—in the persons' consciousness, will help to expand a person's faith horizon beyond that of his present
world.

The network of meanings that are dominant in a person's life or outlook, make up that individual's world
or horizon. Every person, the most intelligent and the

7*Ibid.,* p. 41.

most ignorant, the most dynamic and the dullest, has a world or a horizon.[8]

The only way a person's horizons can be extended is by the entrance of new meanings into his life—at the consciousness level—so that spiritual growth within the secular world can be realized. This is true because this process relates the person to a "world of spiritual values," given by his faith in God and causing him to struggle for such a relationship through his choices.

Michael Novak points to this truth as he speaks of the horizon which links the person and his "world of values" in a mutually defining relationship:

> What we know of the world is known only through consciousness, and we are conscious only through being in a world. Self and world interpenetrate; neither exists in regard to the other until they are mutually united in act. One pole of my horizon is the range of all I can experience, understand, evaluate and do. The other pole is the subject of these activities of experiencing, understanding, evaluating and doing. Neither pole can be attended to without reference to the other.[9]

Thus, within the ministry of spiritual counsel, the task of the pastor is precisely to create such a "horizon" by uniting the one pole, the person, and the other pole, the values of the Chirstian faith; but this can only be done by "cutting into" the current secular world-view with this "network of Christian meanings."

We are not merely speculating here in "metaphysics"; the pastoral task remains practical! This consciousness level, which creates new horizons, must be created through those elements within which the Christian person lives every day: the Christian community (including scripture, sacraments, models, prayer, all of which make up that community), books,

[8]*Ibid.*, p. 34.
[9]Michael Novak, *The Experience of Nothingness* (New York: Harper and Row, 1970) p. 27.

parents, spouses, etc. After all, a world, and its horizons, is constructed of the meaningful *relationships* in which that person exists, and of the *patterns* within which he makes his choices. The pastor who ministers to persons who come to him for counsel cannot forget (as the secular world-view might want him to so forget) that there is no objective fact (or happening or circumstance, etc.) which stands by itself; we are always being influenced and educated by some*thing* or some*one*—and if not by our Faith, then by something else. This does not mean that there are no objective facts (good and bad) which seek to influence people; what is important is not these facts, but the Christian person's *attitudes* toward them, his *perception* of what they mean, and his *intentions* in the face of such facts. This is why the pastoral task must remain focused on "meanings," those intended to stimulate growth and to create Christian horizons toward which the pastoral counselor can lead persons. The challenge of the pastor in confronting a secular world-view, then, is not one of denying the objective facts which are known by experience, but, as soon as there is an acknowledgment of such facts, to lead the Christian to ask, "what does this mean?" Thus, the Christian fights his spiritual warfare; the world is challenged without denying its reality, good and bad. Horizons must be established on the ground upon which that person stands, and in the present time of that particular circumstance.

We cannot, however, by-pass the pastor's *own* horizons. Lauder states this in a most practical way:

> In trying to stay in dialogue with Christian meaning, a priest has various sources that can help him. Some of these are Christian revelation, scripture, the teaching Church, the sacraments, prayer, spiritual reading, his fellow priests, and the Christian community. A priest tries to sustain a Christian horizon not only for himself. His vocation is to try to help others sustain a Christian horizon. Thus he models his life after that of Jesus.[10]

[10]*Op. cit.,* Lauder, p. 41.

3. Freedom in the Secular World

The second aspect in the establishment of a network of Christian meanings is *freedom*. Here we are interested only in what such a quality means in terms of the ministry to persons. This is necessary because within the secular world-view there seem to be two modes (and a large variety of "schools" which are built upon these two modes) of dealing with human freedom: *determination* and *uninhibited arbitrariness*. The person who comes to the pastor for counsel will often believe that one of these two speaks of both his predicament and his options. But the truth is that the pastor can accept neither. This concern for freedom is important because freedom takes its value from Christian commitment and responsibility, and here, *choice* is crucial. *Determinism* misses completely the human element and mystery since the choices are already decided by outside factors; *arbitrariness* ("feelings," what makes me "happy," etc.) overlooks, among other things, the reality of influences in the person's life. In both cases the element of choice is aberrant. Christian freedom does not say that there are no influences—historical, cultural, educational, etc.—which seek in various ways to "determine" the person in his situation. What it does say, however, is that the Christian person is free to choose how he will relate to such influences and necessities. The Christian consciousness is defined, not by denying realities, but precisely by *taking a stand in the light of the realities*. Here faith enters consciousness.

Furthermore, this Christian view of freedom is not disconnected from the previously mentioned "horizon"; one has the freedom to struggle toward the faith horizon. These two, freedom and the horizon, are tied together by the Christian consciousness, and in fact, make up the heart of the network of meanings in which the person can grow within the secular world-view.

Each time a person acts, he or she goes beyond what he or she was before the action. Each time a person

acts, he or she throws himself or herself into the
future ... The choices that persons make move them
in a particular direction.[11]

By leading persons to choices in their everyday life,
choices which are forthcoming from a true Christian consciousness, such persons are moved in the direction of growing
toward God (*Theosis*).

4. Truth in the Secular World

In the ministry to persons who live in a secular world,
truth is the crucial aspect. Truth tells persons the most important meanings about themselves, others and God. For
the Christian, truth tells us who God is and who we are.
It is concerned with *relationships*. Christian truth is revealed
in the model of Christ, in whom we understand both the
ultimate meaning of humanity and the meaning of divinity;
thus Christ is *the Truth*. ("He who has seen me has seen
the Father"—Jn 14:9.)

The main thrust of the pastor's responsibility in leading
persons to growth is to reveal the truth about the meaning
of that person's life and circumstance in which he relates to
God and his fellows. Ultimately, the truth of Christ must be
brought to bear upon that particular person's meanings.
This must be the basis for how the pastor handles the truth
within the person's life. Needless to say, this can be very
painful: "But now you seek to kill me, a man who has told
you the truth which I heard from God" (Jn 8:40).

Thus the pastor must use Christ as the perfect model
in creating the Christian consciousness, and thus, in applying truth to the person's circumstance. In fact, if he does
not ultimately do this, i.e. apply Christ to the person he
ministers to, Jesus becomes a "divine fact"—*information*—
to be "taken into account," rather than God's wonderful
revelation which speaks to every person. In fact, if the
person is not ultimately led to this truth regarding God and

[11]*Ibid.*, p. 69.

neighbor, he (and the pastor) can only fall prey to the "father of lies."

> Why do you not understand what I say? It is because you cannot bear to hear my word. You are of your father and your will is to do your father's desires. He was a murderer from the beginnning, and has nothing to do with the truth, because there is no truth in him . . . he is a liar and the father of lies. (Jn 8:43)

The pastor knows that such a "battle" against falsity and lies is being waged, even if the secular world-view has created an atmosphere in which this fact is easy to forget. This is the context in which the pastor must lead the person to see his own actions.

As an aspect in the ministry of counsel, the pastor sees the lack of truth precisely in relationships. This, for example, may show itself in a misunderstanding of what "love" is; in a wrong interpretation of what "sin" is between persons; in not properly understanding "guilt" when one transgresses another (either no guilt or inappropriate guilt); in the wrong kind of "anxiety"; in "despondency," etc. In each case, truth must be the criterion for right relationships.

One of the most common problems with regard to truth and relationships, for example, comes in the following way: pastors often make the mistake, in a premature attempt to relieve the pain and guilt which the person has, of rushing in with the reassurance of forgiveness before the contrition and repentance has run its course in the act of confession. Painful as it is to bring the person into the consciousness of the truth, the pastor has the duty to help the sinner to face the full scope of what has happened:

> The painful sharing of the guilt opens the person to receive the gift of forgiveness. If this sharing is interrupted by a premature offering of the gift, the opening process is impeded. Also we pastors may not realize all that is included in our reassurance. Since the confessee has not had the opportunity to share the

whole story, the absolution he or she receives may remain too abstract to be healing.[12]

The other common way the truth is missed in the ministry to persons, is just the opposite of that just mentioned. This happens when the person feeds on attention and pity; he will not "release," and prefers to hold on to anxiety.

> After expressing it, one needs to let go of it—in religious language, to surrender it to God. Because of habit patterns, this may be difficult ... Jesus' words, "Do not be afraid, only believe," can be personalized by the pastor to the anxious sufferer. Paul's exhortation, "Let the peace of God rule in your heart," indicates that we tend to resist God's peace. Anxiety's hold on us is also our hold on it.[13]

In both cases the truth of the Christian faith is at stake and must be brought into the person's predicament by the pastor. This final truth the pastor remembers from Psalm 103:12: "As far as the east is from the west, so far does he remove our transgressions from us."

The last example has to do with facing the truth in the relationship between God and the person. Besides the obvious faith implications of this relationship (e.g. prayer, charity, repentance, sacraments, etc.), the pastor is continuously brought face-to-face with the person's *protest*. Here we mean the response of the person to unwarranted, unjustified suffering. This is the "Jobian protest," the "why" protest, i.e. why is this happening to me? Here the pastor must realize that the "why?" is *not* a question which seeks information or an answer. In this case, the truth relates to the pastor's understanding of what is really happening with this person who so "protests." The pastor (whose presence is perhaps as important, if not more important, as his words) must realize that this may be the *only* way a person can attempt to describe where he is as he stands in the presence of

---

[12]William Hulme, *Pastoral Care and Counseling* (Minneapolis, Minn.: Augsburgh Publishing House, 1981) p. 121.
[13]*Ibid.*, p. 118.

God. In his affliction, "The protest may be one's only genuine
response at the moment to what is happening in one's life."[14]
(It is in this sense, that Jesus cries, "My God, my God, why
hast thou forsaken me?" Ps 22.) Like Job himself, then, the
person "uttered what I did not understand" (Job 42:3), but
it is a true utterance and is a needed step toward the final
"faith step." The pain is, at that moment, uttered "with
sighs too deep for words," and by which only the Spirit
intercedes for us (Rom 8:26).

In such a case, this protest can eventually become a step
toward faith if it is transformed into prayer. The *protest*:
"Does it seem good to thee to oppress, to despise the work
of thy hands and favor the designs of the wicked?... Thy
hands fashioned and made me; and now thou dost turn about
and destroy me" (Job 10:3,8); the *prayer*: "I believe: help
my unbelief" (Mk 9:24). This St Paul meant when he wrote
that in the end, no matter what comes, no matter what
one understands or does not understand (for Job is finally
satisfied when God asks him, "Where were you when I laid
the foundation of the earth" and his response, "Behold I lay
my hand on my mouth"—Job 38:4; 40:4), no matter "if we
live or die ... we walk by faith, not by sight" (2 Cor 5:7).

In this case, the "truth" is that we do have human limits
and this is only too painfully clear. But hope is the Christian's, precisely because in the Incarnation these limits have
been penetrated by Christ, through whom these same limits
can now become possibilities. As Peter finally says: "Lord,
to whom shall we go? You have the words of eternal life"
(Jn 6:68).

This, then, is the final truth which the pastor brings to
the person in his secular world-view: spiritual growth is realized out of a faith in God in which our all too human
limitations can become themselves *possibilities!* "My grace
is sufficient for you, for my power is made perfect in
weakness" (2 Cor 12:9).

[14]*Ibid.,* p. 142.

CHAPTER NINE

The Person of the Pastor

We conclude this study by focusing specifically on the pastor's own growth and identity. In a certain sense, this last section is presented as an epilogue, because it contains some of the crucial aspects of the ministry which have not themselves been the "subject" of our concern. Although particular attention is given to the pastor (clergy), obvious connections can be made in the ministrty of the laity (not to speak of the need for laypersons to truly understand the person of his or her pastor!).

1. The Distinctive Role of the Christian Pastor

It is necessary to begin by describing the distinctive identity of the pastor. We begin this with a criticism which is not unlike the one in the previous chapter; in this case, however, the criticism is directed to the pastor himself and the divorce of his role from its distinct Christian roots and calling.

Why has this divorce happened? It has happened, first of all, because the theology which is so obvious in worship is absent in his counsel and direction, therefore causing a "shift" in the base of ministry. As the pastor or pastoral counselor becomes more proficient in counseling, the theological force is replaced by a psychological base. Consequently, "ministry" is shaped by psychology, rather than ministry shaping all else that may be proper and helpful to the people of the Church (including psychology, if we mean by that term, thinking, acting, behaving, growing, educating, developing, etc.).

Secondly, there are some today who have tried to counter this development by providing "religious parallels" to support what they are doing; in effect, they merely add religious words and acts to their counseling.[1] Since this is but a shallow application and does not change the essence of the counseling, a deeper integration into the theological "base" is needed (what we have called the consciousness-level intrusion). This deeper integration, which such a shallow accommodation simply can not accomplish, takes place only in the pastor or counselor himself, i.e. within his *own person,* thus enabling it to be expressed in the *act* of his counseling.

Thirdly, the picture has become so confused that the distinction has been lost between pastoral care and pastoral counseling. Care does not only mean counseling![2] Pastoral care implies all the shepherding aspects of "caring" and "nurturing"—including the various functions of administering the Word and the Sacraments—which can not be restricted to the treatment of "problems." Pastoral counseling, however, is a "dialogic" function, which is aimed mostly at *growth* through the varying crises requiring preventative, supportive or confrontational types of counseling (see Appendix A); such counseling (direction, guidance) has a more specific function, a narrower base.

The proper "title" under which both care and counseling is to be placed is the *Pastoral Ministry.* "Ministry" is the proper framework because it includes both caring and counseling, it prevents those reductions found in the "either-or" situation, and it certainly includes the ministry of the laity. In addition, "theology" is implied in this word "ministry."

Finally, this lack of clarity increases when the issue centers on "whether or not" to use religious symbols. For the Christian, it is not a question of "whether or not" faith resources are to be used in the ministry, but it is always a

---

[1]William Hulme, *Pastoral Care and Counseling* (Minneapolis, Minn.: Augsburg Publishing House, 1981) p. 8. Hulme also carries this argument into the distinction between "care" and "counseling" in an attempt to demonstrate what is uniquely "pastoral' in the ministry.

[2]*Loc. cit.*

question of "how and when" they can be properly used. If in times past, such religious symbols or faith resources have been misused, the only response can be that one does not correct misuse by disuse, but rather by proper use!

What all this means for our present concern in describing the distinctive Christian role of pastor, is that we have either forgotten our true role, or abdicated it in favor of roles which are totally secular (which some well-intentioned "religious persons" use with a "Christian" label). In this way, various false dichotomies have been created and have led to the disappearance of the distinctly Christian way of ministering to others within the Body of Christ.

Certainly it is time for the Church, through her understanding of the pastoral ministry, to reverse this trend, i.e. of accepting, on the one hand, an uncritical accommodation to secular thought (and especially secular therapy) in the pastoral ministry; and on the other, a false piety (or perhaps an academic theology) which hardly comes to terms with the reality of flesh and blood.[3]

In attempting to discover this distinctive role of the pastor in the Christian ministry, there are two sources to which we can point immediately as examples, each of which speaks about the person of the pastor.

The first is found in the person of Moses, as his ministry is described in Exodus 18. The entire chapter, which is about Moses and his father-in-law, Jethro, reveals certain principles which are important to our understanding today. These principles define the person of the pastor.

In that chapter, the Israelites were camped at the foot of Mount Horeb. Jethro comes to pay a visit to his son-in-law Moses. They have a wonderful conversation in which Moses explains to Jethro the incidents of how they escaped from the Pharaoh, all the travail that came upon them, and finally, how the Lord had delivered them, etc. "Blessed be the Lord . . ." is the response of Jethro.

After this conversation, Jethro becomes distressed with his son-in-law. He discovers that Moses, at this point, was spending the entire day just sitting and listening to the complaints

---

[3]Cf. Alexander Schmemann's points at the beginning of Chapter Four.

of people and issuing judgments on them: "And the people
stood about Moses from morning to evening," as he sat before them to "judge" (Ex 18:13).

Jethro then offers some advice to his son-in-law. Jethro
says:

> "You and the people with you will wear yourselves
> out for the thing is too heavy for you; you are not
> able to perform it alone" (Ex 18:18).

And he quickly adds:

> Listen now to my voice; I will give you counsel and
> God be with you! You shall represent the people
> before God, and bring their cases to God. . . . More-
> over choose able men from all the people, such as
> fear God, men who are trustworthy . . . place such
> men over the people . . . And let them judge the
> people at all times.   (Ex 18:19-22)

And so it was done. Jethro counselled Moses, Moses
counselled these "able men" as "rulers of thousands, of
hundreds, of fifties, and of tens" (Ex 19:21), and these able
men counselled the people.

The point here is the identity of those who are chosen
to minister; they are men who "fear God," who are "trust-
worthy" and are available "at all times." The principle
stated in this text, indeed the entire context and its message,
is an outstanding example that speaks of the person of
the pastor.

The second example which explains the distinctive Christian role of the pastor is found in the words of the Orthodox
Liturgy. Here we refer to the Liturgy of St Basil, and more
specifically to the Anaphora Prayer. In this example we see
the wholeness preserved, i.e. the "whole picture" about
which we have spoken earlier. In this prayer, the liturgy and
the life of the people are held together, and the ministry
of the Church is thus presented in its totality. Remembering
the context of this prayer, the Holy Gifts are offered and
consecrated, as the Holy Spirit is called down "upon us and

these Gifts here offered." Then being called into communion
with "the Forefathers, Fathers, Patriarchs, Prophets, Apostles,
Preachers, Evangelists, Martyrs, Confessors, Teachers, and
every righteous spirit made perfect in faith," those celebrants
present (clergy and laity) are given a "liturgical guide to
the pastoral ministry" as the prayer asks God to:

> Maintain their marriage-bond in peace and concord;
> rear the infants; guide the young; support the aged;
> encourage the fainthearted. Collect the scattered, and
> turn them from their wandering astray . . . set at liberty
> those who are vexed by unclean spirits . . . defend the
> widows; protect the orphans; free the captives; heal
> the sick; . . . those who are under trial, in the mines,
> in exile, in every tribulation, necessity and danger . . .

If the Lord is called upon, through his Body, to be so
"mindful" of such persons, then the role of the pastor or
counselor who ministers as an instrument of Christ, is no less.

These two examples serve well to describe the distinctive
Christian role of the person of the pastor.

2.   The Pastor as Reconciler and Sufferer

The second characteristic of the person of the pastor is
that which revolves around his efforts at *reconciliation,* and
the *suffering* which often accompanies such efforts. If, in
the ministry of the Church, the pastor will be a "reconciler,"
he will suffer. Psalm 119 speaks of this suffering: "It is good
for me that I was afflicted, that I might learn thy statutes"
(Ps 119:81). We read also in Maccabees: "Now I urge
those who read this book not to be depressed by such
calamities, but to recognize that these punishments were
designed not to destroy but to discipline our people" (2
Macc 6:12).

Indeed, such suffering is not for ruin. It is St Peter who
urges the pastor to follow Christ by suffering as he did:

If when you do right and suffer for it, you take it patiently, you have God's approval. For to this you have been called, because Christ also suffered for you, leaving you an example, that you should follow in his steps.   (1 Pet 2:20-21)

If the servant is not above the Master who washed the disciples' feet, he cannot be above the same Master who suffers. In the Book of Acts, we see that this very suffering was the sign of his service (ministry). We are reminded that after Peter cured the cripple at the temple gate, he addressed all Christians, saying:

Men of Israel, why do you wonder at this, or why do you stare at us, as though by our own power or piety we had made him walk? The God of Abraham and of Isaac and of Jacob, the God of our fathers, glorified his servant Jesus, whom you delivered up and denied in the presence of Pilate, when he had decided to release him. . . . . And in his name, by faith in his name, has made this man strong . . . But what God foretold by the mouth of all the prophets, that his Christ should suffer, he thus fulfilled. (Acts 3:12-18)

Peter's reference to "what God foretold by the mouth of all the prophets" is clearly related by Isaiah:

I gave my back to the smiters, and my checks to those who pulled out the beard; I hid not my face from shame and spitting. For the Lord God helps me; therefore, I have not been confounded, therefore I have set my face like a flint, and I know that I shall not be put to shame.   (Is 50:6-7)

When tribulation comes to the one who ministers to the Body (and it *will* come!), it will be for him what he makes of it: either a test or a damnation. This, Somerset Maugham did not understand when, in *Moon and Sixpence,* he said the following: "It is not true that suffering ennobles the character; happiness does that sometimes, but suffering, for the most part, makes men petty and vindictive." What he forgot is the *antecedent* faith and service that is there to greet that suffering which, after all, falls on the just and unjust alike.

Focusing on this problem of suffering, St Augustine says:

The trials of this world are not a stumbling block for the good: be just, and they will exercise you in virtue. When tribulation comes, it will be for you precisely, what you desire to make of it—either a test or damnation ... Tribulation is a fire; has it found for you gold? If so, remove the dross. Has it found for you straw? If so, it will turn you to ashes.

(*Sermon* 81:7)

But Somerset Maugham would be right if we forget that for which the pastor suffers. Suffering may mean nothing in itself, and in fact, it may even be demonic. But for those who minister and those who are served by this ministry, the meaning is crucial, especially in terms of the effort at reconciliation. St Paul points to Christ's act, saying: "All this is from God, who through Christ reconciled us to himself and gave us the ministry of reconciliation ... We beseech you on behalf of Christ, be reconciled to God" (2 Cor 5:18,20). And Paul adds: "[Christ] has now reconciled in his body of flesh by his death, in order to present you holy and blameless and irreproachable before him" (Col 1:22).

To be reconciled with God always involves a change of relationship in which the pastor becomes less and less a stranger, and more and more, a brother in the suffering and death of Jesus Christ. To be reconciled, then, means to assume the death of Jesus Christ as St Paul meant it: "And he died for all, that those who live might live no longer for themselves but for him who for their sake died and was raised" (2 Cor 5:15). The suffering of the pastor, then, is a suffering offered in behalf of Jesus Christ, and not for himself, for it is God who, by grace and communion, reconciles. We are to be agents of that reconciliation, and if that is true, it is only because we know that our suffering is the very suffering of Christ in our own lives, the suffering of which we are but instruments. In line with this, Augustine again speaks:

> Four things are to be considered in every sacrifice: *by* whom it is offered, *to* whom it is offered, *what* is offered, and for *whom* it is offered. Therefore, the same one and true Mediator Himself reconciled us with God by the sacrifice of peace, in order that we might 1) remain one with him (the Father) *to* whom it was offered, 2) in order to make those *for* whom it was offered one in Himself, and 3) in order that *He Himself* (Christ) might be both the one who offered and the one who was offered.
>
> *(The Trinity,* 4:14-19)

Secondly, the Cross is in the center of our suffering and reconciliation. As such, we can only say with St Paul: "But far be it from me to glory except in the cross of our Lord Jesus Christ, through whom the world has been crucified to me and I to the world" (Gal 6:14). And as a command to the pastor: "He who does not take his cross and follow me is not worthy of me" (Mt 10:38).

This, then, is the second decisive characteristic of the person of the pastor: he is a person of reconciliation and suffering, and, as such, is in a decidedly organic relationship with the life, death and resurrection of Jesus Christ. However, only as the reconciler of others to Christ, will he be reconciled himself; to be otherwise, would place him among "the physicians of others, while we are swarmed with ulcers ourselves."[4]

---

[4]Seraphim Papacostas, *Repentance* (Athens: Zoe Publishers, 1970) p. 14.

3. The Pastor and Prayer

Our third and decisive concern is the pastor's personal life of prayer. We must begin by stating very clearly that in the contemporary ministry, there are many "good" pastors. But goodness is not vision, nor growth. Holiness is. It is not in human "perfection," nor in the absence of human weakness, that the pastor is to be judged. His judgment will be based on his pursuit of the way of Jesus Christ, in his whole life—even in the way he reads, strives, hopes, loves, celebrates, etc.—until, despite his weaknesses which may always remain, he is so close to Jesus' "garments" that he becomes a reflection of the person of Christ. On this the pastor will be judged.

But to be that close, he must pray as Christ prayed. With this concern in mind, we turn to the gospel of St Mark to see the pastor's life of prayer in the light of Jesus' prayer life and ministry.

St Mark's gospel, unlike the other Synoptic Gospels, thrusts us at once into the adult life of Christ. Mark does this by first introducing John the Baptist, and then showing our Lord coming to John to be baptized. After John is imprisoned, Mark tells us that Jesus began his Galilean ministry. In the very first chapter we are already introduced to his prayer life *vis-a-vis* his ministry. It is the only Gospel that covers one twenty-four hour time period in Jesus' life, which we will follow in the subsequent verses:

Chapter 1:31. Jesus goes with the two pairs of brothers, Peter and Andrew, James and John, to the home of Simon Peter's mother-in-law. She is ill with fever. Jesus "came and took her by the hand and lifted her up, and the fever left her; and she served them." His healing here is an act of ministry.

Chapter 1:33. It is evening, and many sought Jesus, so that "the whole city was gathered together about the door." People possessed, people with diseases came, and he healed those "who were sick with various diseases, and cast out many demons." Here is clearly the impression of a very "busy" Jesus, ministering late into the night. But then there is the following:

Chapter 1:35-37 "And in the morning, a great while before day, he arose and went out to a lonely place, and there he prayed." And, of course, Simon and the disciples, when they arose later, wondered what happened to him. They finally found him, in his place of prayer and said to him: "Everyone is searching for you," reminding him that he has "work," i.e. ministering to do.

Chapter 1:38. Here one must read very carefully to see what is our Lord's response to the previous, almost accusatory, statement. Jesus ignores their implied question: perhaps they did not yet understand. Instead he merely responds: "Let us go on to the next towns, that I may preach there also; for that is why I came out."

Jesus went off by himself *to pray!* In terms of the ministry, one cannot miss the context: he had a very busy day so that he was working—ministering—well into the night. And now, after he is found, he will have another busy day. But between these busy days, "in the morning, a great while before day," he slipped off to a solitary place in order to pray

Of course, this chapter of Mark's gospel is not the only one in which we find Christ's prayer and ministry related. We turn now to chapter six. Here we find Jesus withdrawing to his own countryside, with his disciples following him. Those that heard him preach and teach in the synagogue wonder how he came to this spiritual insight.

Chapter 6:2. They are saying, "What is the wisdom given to him? What mighty works are wrought by his hands!"

Chapter 6:8. Then he is found explaining to the disciples how they are to preach and teach, that is, "with no bread, no bag, no money," to go with only "a staff"; in short, "to take nothing for their journey."

Chapter 6:12,13. The disciples, in fact, *go out,* doing what he tells them. Here, a remarkable thing happens. St Mark continues this story no further, but inserts the story of the Beheading of John the Baptist. While we read this story of John, the disciples are out doing what Jesus commanded them.

Chapter 6:30. After a space of time (during which the story of John is related), the disciples return and are excited to tell the Master all the wonderful things they have done in their ministry. Again we find Christ ever so gently, taking his disciples aside.

Chapter 6:31. "And he said to them, 'Come away by yourselves to a lonely place, and rest a while.' " Jesus draws them away because he knows the importance of this intimate connection between *prayer and ministry.* This is no less true for those in the ministry of the Church: the closet and the altar, the private prayer and the public ministry, must never be separated.

Of course, Christ and the disciples were "hassled," as is the pastor of today. The people knew, in fact, where they were going, and even went there before them! In verse 33, we find them waiting for Christ and the disciples. Finally, after ministering to the multitudes by feeding them, he again made his disciples get into the boat and go before him to the other side, to Bethsaida, while he dismissed the crowd. "And after he had taken leave of them, he went up on the mountain to pray" (Mk 6:45-46).

It is difficult to miss the point of St Mark's gospel, especially its relevance to those who minister: the more occupied Jesus is with ministry and preaching, the more he speaks in prayer to his Almighty Father.

The contemporary pastor also must deal with people, with administration, meetings, activities, etc., which are part of his ministry. But if the person fails to step aside, to enter the "lonely place" of his individual prayer life, i.e. his "closet," his ministry will be no more than that of a "handyman" who is there to ease the pains of his flock's daily problems. In such a case, this pastor will not "be steady, endure suffering (nor will he) do the work of an evangelist, and fulfill (his) ministry" (2 Tim 4:3-5).

These, then, are some of the references which speak of the person of the pastor. These sources are certainly not exhaustive, and much more needs to be written about this last concern. This chapter was included in order to focus on a number of "remnants" that were only mentioned in the previous chapters. Other important qualities, e.g. the pastor's *congruence* (in which he maintains an inner identity of strength), his capacity for *acceptance* (not approval) and compassion, etc., have been thoroughly discussed elsewhere.

It needs only to be added that the person of the pastor must be a reflection of what the prophet Isaiah knew of God Himself: "And his name will be called Wonderful Counselor" (Is 9:6).

Our thoughts on this "ministry" must end, not with our own words, but with those of St Symeon the New Theologian who directly addresses this ministry of the Church:

> If anyone will say that some of those who are like this, explain divine scripture, theologize, preach orthodox doctrine, let them know that it is not in this that the work of Christ consists ... The Son of God, the Logos, did not become man in order only that men should believe in the Holy Trinity, glorifying it, theologizing about it, but to destroy the works of the devil.[5]   (Homily 10:4)

This is followed by an even more precise word to those who minister:

> To those of you who have received the faith of Christ, the works of the devil shall be destroyed; to him may be entrusted the mysteries of theology and the orthodox faith.[6]

And finally, St Symeon recalls for those in the ministry of the Church what King David of old calls the "sackcloth": "Thou didst rend my sackcloth and didst gird me with gladness, that my glory may chant to Thee, and that I may not be pierced with sorrow" (38th Homily).[7] By this

---

[5]Saint Symeon the New Theologian, *The Sin of Adam; Seven Homilies* (Platina, CA: St Herman of Alaska Brotherhood, 1979) p. 48, Hom. 10:4.
[6]*Loc. cit.*
[7]*Ibid.*, p. 61. Hom. 38.

"sackcloth," St Symeon means our own corruption and death. We are all "ordained," whether in baptism or as clergymen, to carry this message: the sackcloth has been removed. We have been given gladness. For that, God must be blessed, and those who minister in his name must be blessed.

Thus, we offer this prayer of blessing for those in the ministry of the Church: "Blessed be the God and Father of our Lord Jesus Christ, the Father of mercies and the God of all comfort, who comforts us in all our affliction, so that we may be able to comfort those who are in affliction" (2 Cor 1:3-4).

Appendix

Some Practical Concerns

Earlier, in Chapter 9, it was mentioned that the pastor is a person who must prevent, support, and confront. In each of these roles, his hope must continue to be for growth on the part of those to whom he ministers. The following outlines are offered as an addendum in which one can see the practical situations in which the pastor is such a person. Taken from the Liturgical and Pastoral Institute at St Vladimir's Seminary in the summer of 1980, they project the basic types of Pastoral Ministry: *Preventative, Supportive and Confrontational.* These types of ministry are followed by some scriptural references that the pastor may use in guiding those entrusted to him. They are best used in the context of the chapters on The Ministry of Spiritual Counsel.

Basic Types of Pastoral Ministry

I. Preventative Ministry

Goals
1) To anticipate problems before they arise.
2) To prevent worsening of existing problems.

Examples
1) Young people facing marriage.
2) Providing guidance principles for spiritual "defenses."
3) People facing separation crises (various kinds, e.g., divorce or death of spouse).
4) People facing surgery or serious illness.
5) People facing moves or retirement, etc. . . .

228

Pastoral Response
1) Being alert to potential problems and dangers, *to begin with!*
2) Confronting persons with possible dangers.
3) Education in discussion, visitation, sermons, etc. . . .
4) Being tactful (cf. Sts Chrysostom, Basil, John of Kronstadt, Cosmas Aitolos).
5) Encourage trustful discussion (e.g., as Father Confessor).
6) Be alert to helpful Scripture and other reading material.

Possible Dangers
1) Ignoring the potential problem until it becomes serious.
2) Overdramatizing, making the problems sound worse than they are.

II. Supportive Ministry

Goals
1) To undergird, hold up or stabilize troubled persons.
2) To help the *person himself* gain strength to cope with his problem, etc. . . .

Examples
1) Serious illness in the person or the family.
2) Death of loved one.
3) Break-up of marriage or engagement.
4) Rejection by a significant person.
5) Characteristics such as inadequacy, immaturity, over-dependency, consistent failure, etc. . . .

Pastoral Response
1) Being a "shoulder to lean on," i.e., reassuring, comforting, encouraging, guiding, etc. . . . (*poimena* and and *episkopos* concept).
2) Encouraging the person to *face* his problem and "grow" from it ("Every obstacle is for the good").
3) Help to give a true and objective view of the situation.

4) Help to build spiritual defenses, e.g., confidence to "make it," "to enter the arena of life" (Chrysostom), "put on the armor of Christ" (St Paul), etc. . . .
5) Discuss the "meaning" of the person's problem.
6) Be alert to helpful Scripture and other reading material.

Possible Dangers
1) Overdependency by the person on the pastor, e.g., see goal #2 above.
2) Encouraging the person toward fruitless self-pity, "wallowing" in his problem, dwelling too much on his feelings, etc. . . .

III. Confrontational Ministry

Goals
1) To force the person to face and deal with some sin or difficult situation.
2) To help the person to develop moral strength to avoid similar problems in the future.

Examples
1) Any immoral or sometimes illegal action, e.g., drug use, promiscuous sexuality, etc. . . .
2) Actions which cause guilt feelings.
3) Actions which Church and Scripture consider wrong.

Pastoral Responses
1) Confronting person with reality of the situation, if he is trying to "talk around it."
2) Encouraging Confession to God and to Father Confessor, with assurance that God can forgive him, if truly repentant.
3) Supporting and accepting him as a person (acceptance is not approval).
4) Guiding the person toward "restitution" and "change" (*metania*).
5) Encouraging a more responsible way of behaving.

6) Strengthening conscience and self-control (relationship between *behavior* and *motivation*).
7) Be alert to helpful Scripture and other reading material.

Possible Dangers
1) Rejection of the person because of his action, and not the sin.
2) *Excessive* moralizing!
3) *Not* truly facing the issue.
4) Not helping the person to change his behavior.
5) Concentrating too much on "causes and sources" rather than on dealing with the current behavior and relationship, etc. . . .

Some Scriptural References for the Pastoral Ministry

These can be used:
1) By the pastor himself, i.e., in preparing himself.
2) For distribution to the *person* to whom the pastor is ministering, e.g., given by the pastor at the end of some direction or counsel according to the problem, and probably with other material.

Problem	*Scriptural References*
Anxiety and Worry	Ps 43:5; 46:1-2; Prov 3:5-6; Mt 6:31-32 Phil 4:6-1, 19; I Pet 5:6-7.
Anger	Ps 37:8; Jas 1:19; Col 3:8.
Courage	Ps 27-3; 31:24; Prov 3:26; 14:26. Mt 28-20; 2 Cor 5:6; Eph 3:11-17;
Death	Phil 4:13, 2 Tim 1:8-9. Ps 116:15; Jn 14:1-6; Rom 14:8 1 Th 5:9-10; 2 Ti 4:7-8; Rev 21:4.
Discouragement	Ps 27:14; 34:4-8, 17-19; 43:5; Mt 11:28-30; Jn 14:1, 27; 16:33; 2 Cor 4:8-9 Heb 4:16.
Envy	Ps 37:17; Prov 23:17; Rom 13:13; Col 5:26

Problem	Scriptural References
Forgiveness of Sin	Ps 32:5; 51:1-19; Prov. 28:13; Is 55:7; 1 Jn 1:9; Jas 5:15-16.
Hatred	Eph 4:31-32; 1 Jn 1:9; 2:9-11.
Helplessness	Js 34:7 27-5, 24; 55:22; Heb 4:16; 13:5-6; 1 Pet 5:7.
Loneliness	Ps 27:10; Prov 18:24; Jn 15:14; Heb 13:5.
Patience	Heb 10:36; Gal 5:22; Ja 1:3-4; 5:7-8, 11.
Sin	Ps 51; Is 53:5-6; 55:7; 59:1-2; Rom 3:23; 6:23; 1 Jn 1:9.
Temptation	1 Cor 10:12-13; Heb 2:18; Ja 1:2-4, 12; 2 Pet 2:9.
Weakness	Ps 24:14; 28:7; Is 40:29, 31; 41:10; 2 Cor 12:9; Phil 4:13.
Wisdom and Understanding	Prov 4:7; Job (various sections, e.g., 28); Ja 1:5.

(Every pastor can make his own list; these happen to be the ones that I use.)